# TNNS LSSNS

FILLING THE GAPS IN YOUR GAME

## MARCUS PAUL COOTSONA

PRO TENNIS PRESS

# CONTENTS

TNNS LSSNS

Filling the Gaps in Your Game by Marcus Paul Cootsona.

To book Marcus Cootsona for a speaking engagement, ask tennis instructional questions, or secure advice on deep topics of moment and/or import, please contact him at myprotennis@comcast.net.

Cover Illustration by Steven Novak

First Edition

Library of Congress Cataloging-in-Publication Data has been applied for.

ISBN: 978-0-578-41878-0

PRO TENNIS PRESS

P.O. Box 447

Menlo Park, CA 94026, USA

www.marcuscootsona.com

# ALSO BY MARCUS PAUL COOTSONA

## Simpler, Smarter Tennis

Occam's Racquet

## Wally Wilson Mysteries

Slammin'

Rubber Match

## Severin Force Political Thrillers

Initial Force

*FOR MY STUDENTS*

"If you stay ready, you ain't gotta get ready."
– James Brown

# FOREWORD IS FOREARMED

*"What's holding up the delay?"*
Mary Carillo's uncle

It has been seven years since I wrote *Occam's Racquet – 12 Simple Steps to Smarter Tennis* – my effort to make the complex sport of tennis and the needlessly complex activity of instructing the complex sport of tennis understandable and manageable. And less complex.

During the septet of years that followed its publication, I would like to say that I have been living a life of famous-author leisure. But, no, that hasn't exactly happened. Instead, I have continued in the best don't-give-up-your-day-job tradition, of toiling at my day job – teaching tennis to intelligent, engaging, successful individuals on one of the most beautiful private tennis courts in the continental U.S – and writing more words about it.

## AN HONEST DAY'S WORK – PER WEEK

But so no one gets the wrong idea, it hasn't been all stunning clothes, exquisite strokes, and terribly witty bon mots. Not by a long shot.

Okay, well, it mostly has been. But, still, believe it or not, there's real work involved in teaching a leisure activity in shorts in nice weather all day most days of the year. Okay, well, there's work involved. Okay, to be honest, it's actually pretty cushy. But give me some credit. I know it's cushy, and I've reconciled myself to a downwardly-adjusted sense of self-worth. But that isn't really the main thing about it. You see, when I'm not re-applying my sunscreen or checking my hair, I am actually often paying attention to what my students are doing on the court *and* to what they're telling me that they're doing on other courts.

Point being, I think that despite my natural, and, now admitted, tendencies toward sloth, torpor, and vanity, I've learned a few more of the ins and outs of the old game in the last seven years, and have discovered a few more techniques and approaches that I think will help the average or above-average or above-above-average player have more match success, and win more matches. And if you buy, or have bought, this book in one or all of its many formats, you can be the ultimate judge of whether or not that's true. And, if you have, I thank you for your purchase. And your review. When you have a chance, of course.

So what exactly is this book?

**ALL BOOKED UP**

Good question.

The chapters that follow this preparatory prologue of windy, self-congratulatory naval-gazing are a combination, or a rehashing, or an unholy marriage, one of those things, of three sources – articles I have penned in the intervening, previously alluded to hard-at-work years for a defunct, but now perhaps resurrected instructional website, combined skillfully and willy-nilly with articles I wrote that have never seen the light of any website, combined with articles I wrote specifically for this new book.

And so, there it is, the sordid, compacted history of how we got to this point, you and I, but I think that slightly more explanation may be in order. At least in one specific area.

You see, as I was conceiving of this new book (the second one of a tennis instructional trilogy, perhaps?), and blending the many sources mentioned above to facilitate its conception, and factoring in my experience from the wonderful, revealing laboratory that is teaching tennis six days a week from the rooster's crow until the cows' homecoming to write the cute little thing, I took a moment and asked myself, "In the seven years since you last wrote about tennis, what about tennis has changed?"

## THE THINKING PRO'S MAN

And I thought, and I thought, and I thought. (Which is not a typical tennis pro activity.)

And the answer I came up with was – not much.

It is true, of course, that racquet-head head-size has congealed industry-wide to an area of around 100 square inches, give or take. It is also true that the tennis warm-up as we knew it for three decades is mostly gone, replaced by formless fleece hoodies and orphaned baggy pants without leg zippers. And, it is undeniable that polyester strings have become more supple, user-friendly, and widely used. But those are all equipment considerations.

And, sure, it's also true that strokes are taught a little differently now than they were in 2011. We're beginning to see the resurgence, and maybe even the refulgence, of the one-handed backhand. Slice is making a comeback on both sides. Drop shots are trendier on tour than they were in 2011. And serve speeds continue to increase. But those are all minor technical considerations. Stuff that really doesn't factor in any large way into, for instance, winning or losing USTA league matches to one of those 'clubs' that meet on public courts and seem to recruit players from five different states who have all just mysteriously leveled down.

So the question really is – has there been any change in the parts of the game of tennis that really matter to your game? The parts that help you win matches?

I think the answer to that question is a resounding, no. And here's why.

## THE MORE THINGS STAY THE SAME

For the bulk of recreational and league and tournament players, the same concerns they were concerned about in 2011 are the same concerns they are concerned about in 2018 – at least to judge by my interactions with them. In other words, in the most important ways, nothing about how to dominate match tennis has changed. Which is both comforting and a little unsettling. But maybe not in equal proportions.

The strokes that were hard to master in 2011 are still hard to master in 2018. The strategies that proved elusive to execute then are still elusive now. The pre-match preparation and focus that were difficult to establish and maintain are still all as difficult to establish and maintain these many years later. And the ability to wrap it all up into a thirty-thousand-foot overview while contesting a match in real time on a tennis court against a determined junk artist with a pronounced limp and a loud laugh is still tougher to bite into than a three-dollar steak.

To put it bluntly a second time – Nothing in match tennis has changed in the last seven years. Or, the last seventy. And that, again, is comforting and unsettling. Because if you as a player want to get better at winning tennis matches now and in your future, some things need to change.

## QUO TEMDIMUS?

## (WHERE ARE WE GOING, INDEED?)

So, then, how can we change what has not changed, and seems unchangeable?

Well, my friends, that is what we're planning, in the pages that follow, to find out. But before we do, I'm going to ask you to look inward. You see, in order to change the unchanged, you are going to need to figure out what in your personal game needs changing. And, to do that, I suggest asking yourself three questions –

• Can I win matches consistently *with the strokes and match approach that I have*?

• And, if I can't, do I know *what* I need to add to my game to be a consistent winner?

• And, do I know *how* to add what I need?

The three questions above (or, at least, the second and third questions) seem like big asks, I'll admit. But they might be easier to answer than it seems. You see, you're already in touch with the source of the answers. And you confront that source every time you play match tennis, win or lose.

The source is *your game*. But not your lesson game, or your hit–with-friends game. The game we're talking about is your game-game. The game you play against an opponent – a snarling, mean-spirited, win-at-any-costs adversary. (Much like the players on that team that recruits from five states.) The game that counts.

And if you listen to it, your game-game will tell you what it's lacking.

But you need to pay attention. Not only to your shots, but to your entire game, from beginning to end.

And, read this book.

## LE BIG CAVEAT

And, of course, I know and you know, that any instructional book that wants to teach you how to do anything is, by necessity, addressing not what you already know, but what you don't know. What you need to know. We know this. It's why you buy the book. It's just that with the sport of tennis, those things that you don't know how to do and the things that you don't even know you don't know how to do, can compromise the things you can do and do know how to do and do know that you know how to do. You know? That's why putting some introspection and examination into your game-game, your match game, will help you use this book to your ultimate and, we hope, decisive advantage.

## JUSTIFICATION SECTION

So this book is for match players. Specifically, match players who want to win more matches. Players, in short, who are after The FOING. That's right, The FOING.

And what exactly is The FOING?

Glad you asked.

The FOING a technical term of art. (At least in my vocabulary.) And it's a feature you want in your tennis game. And something I yell at the TV when I'm really into watching a particular match.

Here, from an overlooked dictionary, is a definition –

FOING | Foy-yoy-yoy-yoy-yoy-yoing (accompanied ideally by classic Warner Bros. bouncing spring sound effect and pronounced with matching inflection.)

noun (pl. **same**)

a consciousness-jarring, assumption-shifting, paradigm-altering move or event of some sort. Most often in sports competitions.

ORIGIN

early 21st cent.: from individuals observing sports from and upon couches or other upholstered seating units, exclaiming enthusiastically over a particularly significant on-field comeuppance for which no other expression seemed appropriate or adequate.

Yeah, so that's The FOING. You probably had a vague, intuitive sense of it, had it whisper its seductive call to action to your tennis subconscious, but never knew exactly what to call it. Well, it's called The FOING, and it's the desirable xyz-factor for match play success. We've defined it and now we're going to go and grab us some.

This is then, therefore, a book for match players who want to engage The FOING. It is not particularly a book for the many players who don't want to play competitive tennis. (Although I couldn't ever, with a clear conscience, discourage an honest, interested, algorithm-goosing purchase.) But if you are happy hitting the court with a friend and just rallying and that's what you want to get out of tennis, you don't necessarily need to identify and fill in the gaps in your game-game. Why? Because in a rally you can work around your deficiencies. And with no score hanging in any balance, the gaps in your game may not matter very much to your enjoyment. And that's all fine.

But if you want to succeed and wield you some The FOING against an opponent, someone who wants to beat you, someone who isn't on the other side of the court to contribute to your stroke consistency and well-being and your personal fitness, then you need solutions to those things you don't know and don't yet know how to do. To overcome actual opponents, you can't have too many holes in your game. And if you've played for a while, and those holes are still there, you need a detailed method for fixing them.

In other words, you need to *fll n th gps n yr gm*. And not just in your game, but in your game-game (*gm-gm*). And I think I can help you there.

Observing players on a daily basis and working with them to shore up weak areas of their physical and mental games, I realized that the same gaps seemed to yawn through the otherwise proficient games of many highly-skilled, dedicated, well-appointed players as well as players at much lower skill levels. Identifying these gaps and working on replacing them with knowledge, techniques, and purpose seemed like a sensible way to create better match players. And that, my friends, is what we're going to do.

## HOLISTIC MONITOR

Great. So, what kind of gaps are we talking about?

Most every player at every level has gaps in stroke skills to be sure. But, unfortunately, just shoring up strokes is not typically enough of a game-game fix. Great strokes alone don't win matches. If they did, then the top players at every level would be the ones with the best strokes and the best stroke form. And a quick look around will tell you that that just isn't the case. Effective players' strokes all obey at least some tennis fundamentals, but their strokes aren't always their edge in match play. The gaps we're talking about are much more than simple mechanical additions or revisions. The gaps we want to look at are gaps in how you *prepare, plan, and think* about the game.

The total game. The complete game. The winning game.

But, back to me. And my students.

Observing and talking to players with well-honed or at least semi-honed technique who were routinely losing to other players with less than even semi-honed technique, led me to wonder, what are the players in the rough and tumble 'real' world outside the manicured, routinely resurfaced teaching court doing to increase their chances of winning, *before* they play, and *while* they play? And, what are they doing or thinking about *after* they play to integrate what they've learned while playing in order to set themselves up to play better the next time?

Anything?

And, if they are doing *some* things, are they doing the *right* things? And, even if they're doing the right things, should they do *more* things?

In short, what are the common strengths of successful match tennis players that the players who aren't as successful don't yet have, and how can we identify those strengths and put them into *your* game?

Well, here's one answer.

From what I can see, great, successful match players exhibit three primary characteristics –

They are, like, TOTALLY SKILLED.

They are ADAPTABLE.

And they UNDERSTAND AND USE MATCH CONTEXT.

### MAYBE IT'S HAMMER TIME

Boss skills and adaptability may be obvious, and we will talk much more about both ideas, but what do I mean by *understanding and using match context*?

Well, put one way, it means that no matter what you might think, you are not always a hammer on the court and that therefore not every match you play is a nail. Sometimes you're called upon to be the opposite of a hammer. In a particular match, on a particular day, you might need to be a feather. Or a sapling. Or a river. And, or, yes, sometimes, you actually do need to be a hammer, because that is the right approach on that particular day for that particular match. And, in that case, that match is indeed a nail.

But to know if it is a hammer day or not, you must plan *before* you play, and engage your intellect and your powers of observation *when* you play. You need to be flexible in your approach and adjust what you're doing on the match court to the conditions, the opponent, and what your body is able to pull off that day. Every day is a new day in sports, no matter how skilled you are. The MO that worked for the match yesterday, may not be the one that's going to get you el large 'W' today.

Competence creates confidence. And confidence high-fives, chest-bumps, and bro-hugs competence. If you develop serious skills, you will be confident on the court. And gnarly skills allow you to adapt your game in real time with a real result on the line.

Both these attributes will go a long way toward making you better. But neither attribute can ultimately hold sway and lead to a straight-set win if you don't observe, process, and calibrate your game to the conditions at hand. These are gaps that, once filled, will make you a more effective match player, now and in the future.

So we're going to talk all about those three ideas – Mad Skills, Adapt-ability, and Context – and give you some concrete concepts and exer-cises to do and think about that will help you fill the game-game gaps that you didn't even know you had.

Because playing a complete game *before* the match, *during* the match, and *after* the match is the path to successful match tennis.

It always has been.

And it always will be.

## AND SO –

Seven years ago, I wrote *Occam's Racquet* to help you make your tennis simpler and smarter. Today, I offer you this new book to help make your tennis game deeper and rounder.

Deeper, yes. But rounder? That isn't quite it.

Maybe *more well-rounded*?

That's almost it. But still…

To make your game *complete*. That's it. Complete. That was the word.

Complete. I offer you this book to help make you tennis game complete. And The FOING inclusive as well.

And, so, that's my goal for you – a fully realized, complete game, leavened with a robust amount of The FOING potential, using whatever strokes you already have or may develop. A game that will be a winning game on the match courts.

So, enough waiting, already. And enough preamble. It's taken seven years to get this far – not including the additional minutes you've just burned reading this pre-initial nonsense – so let's get to it.

Meet you at the introduction.

### *ADDITIONAL INFORMATION PRESENTED AS A BONUS IN ORDER TO INCREASE PERCEIVED BOOK VALUE –*

Sloth and torpor have gotten a bad rep and a bad rap. Sloth is defined as "reluctance to work or make an effort," and secondarily as "laziness." Torpor is defined as "a state of physical or mental inactivity," and again only secondarily as "lethargy." So we're going to generously choose the first definition in both cases.

I think sloth and torpor used intelligently are powerful tennis weapons. My native sloth has aided and combined with my developing torpor to create athletic efficiency – a true necessity when you're on court slapping spheres eight hours a day.

Channel productive sloth and thoughtful torpor for your strokes and your game. Don't make the game harder than it is or use energy unnecessarily by moving when you don't need to or moving too much. Hit just enough shot to win the point.

# PRIOR TO THE SNAP JUDGMENTS

*"A goal without a plan is just a wish."*
Antoine de Saint-Exupéry.

I hate to see good players lose. Especially when they're players I teach.

Well, maybe hate is too strong a word. And it's an ugly word as well. So, let's say instead that I'm *tired* of seeing good players lose. Tired of seeing it, and equally tired of hearing that it happened.

And I want to fix it. For a number of reasons.

## THE GOOD, THE BAD, AND THE MOONBALL

As a promoter and instructor of aesthetically-pleasing, winning tennis strokes, I just wish that *aesthetically-pleasing* and *winning* would go together more often. For my students. For me and my reputation. And for the game in general.

But they don't always.

And, for better and worse, that's the way a one-on-one sport like tennis can roll. An opponent, with consistently lousy and unpredictable pseudo-strokes, can hornswoggle a well-schooled player who is working to craft his or her game correctly.

It happens on the courts of this great nation all the time – bad strokes and match savvy drowning out elegant, correct strokes, and good intentions. And I hate (and I do mean hate) to see it. But what's the solution? Should we just give up on beautiful strokes, and try to win by any mechanical means possible?

Absolutely!

Just kidding.

Of course we shouldn't. For one thing, what would happen to my job? Right?

## MORAL HIGH GROUND

And there are other arguments for developing sound technique that don't even apply to my livelihood. The most significant being that the only high-percentage path to developing a winning tennis game is through proper technique. Yes, there are abundant 3.0s and 3.5s with poor technique out in the world, but 3.0s and 3.5s they will mostly stay. To advance to 4.0 and beyond, you must hit the ball correctly. Why? Because the quality opponents you play will. And they will beat you.

To play better at whatever your level is and eventually level up and go as high and as far as your talent will take you demands precision and chops. And, maybe as importantly, the only way to really look good at a resort court when other guests walk by and don't know what your score is is with strokes that are successful and score points *on purpose*.

Proper technique is not an option to be added onto strokes that work. Later. Or something. It is the way you build strokes that work efficiently. And it's the way you protect your body so you can play until you're a hundred-and-twenty without a bunch of surgeries or a brace of prosthetic appliances attached to your limbs. It is also a way to add a little more beauty to this world. And that's never a negative. Especially with ugly words like 'hate' being thrown around willy-nilly in instructional books.

So, for all of those good and sufficient reasons, don't give up on them beautiful strokes in your practice or in your matches, okay? Work on them and make them as good and as repeatable in their technical correctness as you can. It's worth it.

But, with all that having been said, the tennis problem, the game-game problem of good strokes losing to lousy ones, is still one for the ages.

Meaning?

Meaning, you may be in full possession of upstanding and proper, like, methodology and a nifty swing and still lose handily to a player who looks like he or she has never had a lesson. Or, to a player with better stamina, or footwork, or strategy, or personal grooming. Or, to a player with lesser stamina, footwork, strategy, and grooming, but with the hackers annoying instinct for keeping the ball in play and making you miss.

And so what are we to do about this? All of it.

Because in some not quite definable meta-way, or something, none of it feels right. Or fair. And seems like no kind of reward for all of your hard work and hourly lesson fees.

So, you may very well be asking, "Okay, then, Mr. Hair-Combed-Sunscreen-Applied-Instructor-Author, what is the darn answer then to this tennis problem for the ages? Huh, palsy?"

**TOUGH LOVE-15**

The answer lies in filling the gaps in your game-game. The gaps that have to do with strokes, of course, but also the gaps that have to do with your preparation, your equipment, your body, your mind, and your senses.

What? All of that, really?

Yaaah. You see, the unspun truth is, whoever you are – your game has gaps. Gaps you can't see. Gaps you may never have considered. Gaps that are making it hard for whatever level technique you have to reliably create comparable or better results. And finding those gaps and filling them in is where the road to more winning will begin.

It's a lot to do and it won't all happen at once. But as soon as you begin to see and think of your tennis game as not just strokes, but as a complete and integrated whole made up of a complementary group of techniques and approaches, you will win matches more regularly – even against those hard-to-play strange-o's with off-putting personal quirks. And that will make you want to add even more technique and approaches. And then a virtuous cycle will begin. Or at least a path to a lot more w's.

You see, though excellent strokes are where great, advanced match tennis starts, you can't go to the court and just grind on strokes and expect to win tennis matches regularly and consistently. As Einstein or Narcotics Anonymous in a 1981 pamphlet or someone else said, "The definition of insanity is practicing the same way over and over and expecting different results." You can definitely plan on the same results if you keep practicing the same things the same way, but if you want your game-game to level up, you have to change what you're doing and how you're doing it.

You need to work also on movement, recovery, fitness, flexibility, commitment, strategy, tactics, awareness, adaptability, and a plan or two or three. And, oh, yes, right, and you need one more thing, too –

creativity. And, yes, I know that's a lot to ask. But tell me the truth, aren't you tired of losing matches to players you *shouldn't* lose to?

I hope the answer is yes. Because, as I said before, I'm tired of it for you. And I want your hard work to pay off. I want you to get you some more and better wins. And some The FOING.

## BUT WHY THIS BOOK?
## (AND NOT SOME OTHER?)

Conservatively, at last count, there were 735 million gaunt, walnut-tan, indifferently-dressed guys (where, by the way, *are* the *women* instructors?) with beige personalities and no vocal technique peddling top spin forehand demonstration videos. But let's be honest, do we really need more forehand instruction?

I mean, is *that* what's holding your game back?

For my students, up through the 4.5 level, it's various things – better fitness, a changed diet, preciser shot placement, and watching the ball into contact to name a few – and rarely is it a stroke problem. For a number of students, knee bend is the issue. They bend their knees in the early stages of a point, but if the exchange goes on past hit five or six, their knees stop inclining. They stand up straight during longer rallies and hit the ball long. And lose the point.

A small sample size of strokes won't show this. Just improving their forehand won't show this. Or fix it. And yet, filling this particular gap (more late-point knee bend) would have enormous consequences for these students for winning more matches. After a certain level, strokes are rarely the match success impediment. It's usually peripheral things. To wit, I spent one tournament summer in the juniors simply concentrating on bending my knees. It didn't have a big effect immediately, but by the end of that summer I was winning more and my quads were ripped. Sort of.

## SO WHO IS THIS BOOK FOR?

This book is for 2.0 to 4.5 players who want to get better at winning matches.

And what about 5.0s?

They can benefit too, but who knows what they'll want to do. Who even knows where they are? As a student once said, "5.0s are like the Yeti. I keep hearing about them, but I've never actually seen one." But they are actually out there in the world, and 5.0s can get better as well. Their games have gaps too. They just may be different, more exotic, more subtle gaps. And they may or may not want to acknowledge them.

## DO I NEED THIS BOOK?

Do you need this book?
I'm not sure you do.
Do you?

Here's a simple question that might provide an answer. If you've ever said to yourself, or a friend, or your dog, or anyone who'll listen, "I keep taking lessons, I keep practicing, but I'm not winning more," then, yes, I think this book could be for you.

## BUT THEN WHY DOESN'T THE BOOK COST MORE?

This book is priced the way it is so many players can buy it and improve.

## WHAT DOES IT LOOK LIKE WHEN IT'S DONE?

And when you read it, and examine your game, work to fill the gaps, and adapt to conditions on the match court, you will win more matches.

## AND SO

So, here's what you need to do. You need to now, as of today, even before you check your email again, or see why the dog is being so quiet, or have another sip of that green smoothie, begin to think about your game-game, your match game, as being made up not just of strokes, but of parts – three parts, to be specific.

PART ONE is what you need to do *before you even arrive at the court*. Maybe even before you buy a racquet.

PART TWO is what you need to do *on the court*.

And PART THREE is analyzing *off the court* how it all worked in real time. Or didn't.

And that's what this book is going to teach you. How to thoughtfully and deliberately manage the three parts of match tennis. And how to construct a complete, intentional, and successful game-game.

So, then, what is the first thing you actually need to do to play better match tennis? The Part One part?

## TELL YOURSELF HOW YOU'RE GOING TO PLAY

Plan.

That's right. School your match game before you even go out to play a match. Or a game.

Plan what you're going to hit. Plan how you're going to hit. And plan what you're going to do if your plan doesn't pan out. And that's not all the plans.

Plan how you will tune up, polish, and just, like, better your strokes. Plan how you will soup up your movement. And plan what you will do to upgrade your fitness and your equipment. In short, think about how you're going to make yourself successful on the court, *before* you actually get on the court. That is to say, think about your game even when you're not playing.

Then, by having done some thoughtful pre-match planning, when you're actually out on the match court, against an opponent who is trying to beat you, you will have a plan that you have already devised that will assist you in your efforts to beat them. Cool, right? As the Scouts of America (formerly, in other times, The Boy Scouts of America) would say, "Be prepared."

As one example, this may mean working on specific drills in lessons or practice sessions where your hitting partner or instructor plays the part of hacker/pusher/weird-stroking opponent and you map out what you need to do to survive the onslaught. But that's only part of the plans.

Because not every opponent will be one of those types.

Some opponents actually do hit consistently produced, predictable, correct shots and will try to defeat you with more power or superior strategy. We call these individuals 'desirable opponents.' And you need to develop tactics and approaches to beat desirable opponents, as well. But, unfortunately, you often need to beat a few of the idiosyncratic, unconventional, arrhythmic goofballs to advance to the people you actually do want to play. So you need to have an approach ready no matter what type of player you draw. And odds are, you need better footwork, conditioning, and stamina to do it.

So, there is much to work on besides raw strokes.

Luck may or may not equal preparation plus opportunity, but winning matches does. So, prepare in practice for the kinds of players you will play for real. All of them.

Lack of ready plans for a smorgasbord of potential opponents is not the only gap many players have, but it's typically the biggest one. And it applies even to players on tour.

## ACTUALLY PLAY

The Part Two part is to take the court, play a match, and see if the plans you've made are the right ones. Employ the specific strokes that you've decided on, pursue the specific strategies you've schemed on, move in the specific ways you drilled, and comport yourself mentally as you've prepared to do. In short, try to play the way you planned. And if that doesn't work, have an alternate plan or two to fall back on.

Because, my friends, there's this –

You may come into the match with a game plan you love, but if that game plan is based on your playing against a player with solid strokes who is offering you some pace to hit back against, and the player you are encountering that day is, instead, one of the soft stroke, strange spin, lob-up-the-center creatures, you will need to be flexible and adjust your game to counter the opponent you are actually playing.

As someone once said, "Reality bites." And so does match tennis.

You are, on any given day, playing against the actual human opponent on the other side of the net, not against an imagined opponent, or against your teaching pro acting as an opponent, or against your hitting partner playing in whatever way he or she usually plays. And this is where you need to be flexible, have some back-up plans, and adapt yourself to the situation. As has been said before, it may or may not be hammer time.

## TELL YOURSELF HOW YOU DID PLAY

And, then, there's the Part Three part. The match is done, and all the executing of plans, the adjusting of plans, and the following of techniques has enabled whatever it has enabled, and the match has ended and has come out however it has come out. And now you enter the after-match mode – the last but not the least important phase of successful match play.

You may have won or you may have lost. And you may be feeling whatever emotions you are feeling, and that's totally groovy. Just remember to take a moment after the match to give yourself some space and time to absorb what has happened, and how you fared with your plans, and then take a few more moments before you leave the well-defined rectangle that is the tennis court, with its rules and etiquette, and re-enter messy, unbounded regular life. And, after taking those moments, give yourself just a jot more time to reflect on and analyze the match and see how you will need to adjust your plans for the next time. Or, maybe, to rejoice in how well your plans worked.

And then?

## CLEANSE AND REPEAT

Go home, stretch, take a shower, hydrate, have something to eat and, if you're so inclined and can do it, take a nap.

And then, as soon as your regular life lets you, get back to working on your game. Because while we care about the product – your wins on the match court – it's the process that gets us there. And it's the dedication, the commitment, the practice hours spent, the tennis instructional books read, and the hourly lesson fees paid in advance by credit card that fuel the process.

## SO, THEN—

In the pages that follow, I'm going to make specific the steps you can take in each of the three parts of the match game to better prepare for your time on court. And, as this is tennis, and not no dental hygienist flossing lecture, you can do it all, or part of it; however much you think you want to do. And so, as with the flossing program you keep meaning to start, but haven't quite gotten to, don't try to do the whole thing at once. Take one step.

Maybe take two steps.

And see what happens with your game.

As a shrink student of mine once said, "People go to therapy when their life as it is becomes more intolerable than the idea of going to therapy." So, even if you're tired of losing to players you *shouldn't* lose to, your tennis life may not quite be intolerable enough yet and you may not be ready to follow every single step I'm going to suggest. And that's fine too. But you bought this book to help you improve, so it makes sense to at least do some of what's in here.

And in case all of that promotion still hasn't moved you to reserve some court time and you need some additional reasons for filling the gaps and improving your game-game, here are a few to consider –

- You will become a better tennis player.
- You will win more matches.
- You will know *how* and *why* you're winning.
- You will become a more popular player.
- You will be invited to play with better individuals often serving tasty refreshments in nice settings.
- Other players will envy your ability. And you. And the quality of your new playing partners and their refreshments and your upgraded match venues.
- You will look better in your tennis clothing. And shoes.

Hope that helped.

So give your chosen steps some time and some run and see if you like the results. As has been said about weightlifting after age 25, or good table manners, or ready cash – any amount will help. Same with improving your match tennis game.

So, in other words, my friends, you don't have to read the whole book. Or read it in order. It's not an all or nothing deal. It's actually more like a menu. And not one of those chef's tasting menus, either, where the house determines what you eat in what order. No, my friends, this is a land-of-the-free, personal-choice-rules à la carte menu where you get to choose what addresses your interests and tastes.

So, go ahead, read a chapter at random and see if you like the suggestions in it. If not, try another chapter.

But, if you're serious about getting better, and writing a detailed Amazon review of this book, do choose something. Your future match tennis success and a broader readership for the author starts with these choices.

So, let's get ourselves over to Part One, shall we?

### ADDITIONAL INFORMATION PRESENTED AS A BONUS IN ORDER TO INCREASE PERCEIVED BOOK VALUE –

You can help yourself right now, in this moment, today by making a list of what gaps there are in your game. Here's one example: For many of my students, better match results would come if they simply got more sleep.

What about you?

You don't even have to list all of them. But you sure can if you want. For a start, try this: What one gap would you fill that would make a difference in your match success? And, yes, of course it can be "buy some wider wristbands." It's your game. And they're your wrists.

# SECTION I

# FOREPLAY

# 1

## LEARNING YEARNING

*"Yearn and learn is what you do. Right on!"*
Earth, Wind and Fire

After the long-winded, interminable double lead-in section where I talked mostly about myself and tried to justify and obscure that fact with an occasional off-hand promise to improve your tennis game, here then is the initial installment of the actual instructional part.

Like, finally.

And the first before-you-hit-the-match-court step to more successful match tennis on-court is *finding an instructor*.

Specifically, a tennis instructor.

An instructor is necessary when you start to learn the game and as you progress, because tennis is not an intuitive game. You can spend days, months, or years alone in felt sphere wilderness, trying to figure out the correct way to produce your strokes and still be shanking squibbers and framing flapjacks. A qualified, professional, well-dressed instructor can streamline the process for faster, more efficient progress and help you build a solid game foundation. And allow you, by hiring them, to perform a vital social service – since most of them can't get jobs doing anything else, anyway.

### DEPENDENT STUDY

But, come on, really, isn't hiring a tennis pro just for rich, country clubbers with Tesla Model Ys who live off carried interest and insider tips? Can't I just do it myself? Like I did with my golf game, that Lobster Thermidor recipe, and that almost level floor in the guest bathroom?

You certainly *can*. But all tennis players can benefit from instruction. And, by extension, all instructors can benefit from tennis players.

Sure, we've all heard the stories about the guy who was a great athlete in some other sport, and who, with no lessons at all, went from zero to tournament-tough 5.0 in eighteen months. Uh huh. Right. Well, send that dude over to the lab, and let's run some tests. Because that dude is clearly not human.

For the rest of us living on planet earth and being subject, as we are, to the laws of physics, not to mention to the exquisite difficulty of mastering the sport of tennis, help and guidance are needed to craft our desired game. Tennis is a complex activity requiring a range of different skills and, again, none of them comes naturally or without counsel and direction.

Wait. What? You mean, hitting a running topspin backhand half-volley can't be learned on my own at the backboard? Or from the Interweb? Or by asking Dave on my USTA team?

A parable might explain it best.

Maybe you've heard about the proverbial room full of typing monkeys, one of whom accidentally pecks out *Hamlet*. Same story here. It might happen that you can experiment your way to stroke competence and lopsided victories, but how long do you have? And keep in mind that, unlike the monkeys, there's only one of you.

So, though we might be able to devise, or happen upon, the correct ways to engineer solid tennis stroke skills on our own, why would we want to? Is it to save a few pesos and instead spend our precious time fumbling about reinventing that which has already been invented, when they are individuals desperately in need of gainful employment who can take us where we want to go much quicker and with much whiter teeth?

Huh? Is that it?

Well, if it is, that's just, as they say, silly. And just makes you the bottleneck in your progress towards better results. Don't set yourself up for failure. Failure's easy enough to find without giving it any push. Instead –

Get professional help.

It will be faster, safer, and the sound technique you will learn will set the stage for vast and lasting progress.

I'm saying this not only because it benefits me and my brethren and sisteren, but because it's the right way to go.

I hope that was convincing.

## PRO FOUND

Anyway, however, the decision to seek instruction is the easy one. The next one – *actually choosing your instructor* – is more difficult and more consequential.

Not only that, but making a sound choice of instructor is subtle. And important. And far-reaching in its consequences. Finding the right instructor *for you* does not necessarily mean reading resumes and checking qualifications. An instructor who can hit like el tour pro will potentially be a much more useful hitting partner than a hit-and-hope intermediate, especially as your game progresses and you need to play practice points against the simulated game of a specific type of player, but don't let that mislead you.

Pedigree does not necessarily matter. Even fabulous ball whacking prowess only matters vitally for playing lessons.

The fact that an instructor was a decorated player with sculpted calf muscles and an unplaceable accent, and has perhaps put in some years on a pro tour may tell you that they know how to play the game at the highest level, but it doesn't necessarily tell you anything about how that person is as an educator or a mentor. Or, if that person can *teach* the game at the highest level for every level of student.

And that's what's important – how the instructor is *as an instructor*. And how that instructor is as an instructor *for you*.

A former touring pro may be an insightful, understanding, and informative teacher, but, often, touring pros and other talent-laden competitive players have lost sight of and lost touch with the difficulties the rest of us encounter when learning the game. Their skills are so well integrated and have become intuitive to such a degree that deconstructing and explaining, in building-block terms, the game for a 2.5 trying to simply coordinate weight transfer and follow through is beyond (or perhaps below) their ability. Again, I'm not saying former pros are incompetent instructors, far from it. But what I am saying is that the qualification 'former pro' is not necessarily the best indicator of qualified current instructor.

And, remember this – it's not about them and their game, anyway, it's about you and your game. They presumably already know how to play, you're trying to learn.

So what about a USPTA certification? Isn't that a way to find a qualified practitioner? Shouldn't a real bona fide professional have five uppercase letters after their name?

Well, a USPTA certification *probably* won't hurt, but the question is: Will it help? Certifications signal that the instructor or practitioner of whatever has met the minimum qualifications to do the whatever they're getting paid to do. Unfortunately, minimums can end up being maximums. And so you have to ask yourself – do you want the minimum daily adult requirement of teaching skill, or do you want an expert? (That was a trick question. I hope…)

When I was a tennis specialty retailer for 163 years or so, earlier in life, I knew a number of company sales reps who were average players and who became USPTA certified pros to meet more contacts and sell more product. Nothing wrong with that. And they were good enough for the minimum required. But as much as I liked them, I wouldn't take a lesson from any of them. Or recommend them.

However, if you need credentials to make you feel comfortable with your instructor choice, go for it. Just don't make that the decider for this decision.

To level up efficiently and spend your lesson money wisely, it's my belief that you want to take lessons from the acknowledged expert, 'The Man' or 'The Woman' in your area. And that person may or may not have a certification. If they've been plying their trade for a few decades, before USPTA was even a gleam in tennis instruction's eye, they may have never gotten or needed the five letters.

So, then, what does matter? What qualifications does a qualified instructor need to have?

## WELL, QUALIFIED?

A qualified instructor needs to know how to *teach*. Preferably tennis. That person needs to be A Teacher.

He or she should understand, given your abilities and tendencies, what the best way *for you* to learn is. Not the way *they'd do it*, or *did it*, or *think it should be done*, but the way *you* can best improve. And this demands a nuanced, non-industrial approach to teaching – meaning not everyone who comes to them gets taught the same minimum daily adult lesson. It takes the ability to construct a specific lesson geared to the specific student on the court with them in that specific hour. And it takes the ability to listen to that student.

So, how do you find a good instructor?

In some ways, the same way you find a good restaurant or investment advisor or bookie. You ask around, interrogate the captive tennis lifers at your local specialty shop, and find out who they've had a good experience with and would recommend. Maybe even read reviews, if there are any. Better yet, ask a friend who's happy with his or her instructor if he or she would recommend that person to you.

And then, pick somebody from the various recommendations who sounds like he or she might be a match with you and take a lesson.

That's right. One single lesson. Just one kick-the-tires session with your new prospective instructor. No commitment beyond that. Participate, judge, and then decide to decide. Evaluate the lesson with your head and your gut and see if your learning style matches up well with the instructor's teaching style.

Take in the instruction, but also stand outside the instruction from time to time and observe the lesson dynamics and interplay between you and the individual you are considering partnering up with. Then, when you're done, and have said thank you for the lesson, and paid that individual for their time, think it over carefully before texting back and booking that second lesson.

If the observations, technical suggestions, and interpersonal situation were groovin' book another lesson. If not, you guessed it, don't book that second lesson.

And if el first lesson wasn't a go, a fit, or a jolly good time, that's okay. Do some more investigating and asking and then take one lesson from somebody else, and maybe somebody else after that, until you find an instructor who speaks to you *and* listens to you.

This is an important relationship. Find that person in your area who is The Man or The Woman of tennis instruction *for you*.

If you want to get better at your chosen sport, you need a partner in the enterprise who shares your goals and views – and is congenial company for an hour or more each week. It's important to get this instructor selection business right. Be discerning. Don't take any wooden placebos.

Because you see my friends, anyone with little shorts, a tan, a large hat, and some red-tinted Oakleys can stand on a tennis court feeding forehands out of a basket of balls and criticize. Anyone can stand on a tennis court and deliver edicts and ultimatums. Anyone can stand on a tennis court and be impatient. Few, however, can stand on a tennis court and consider the student as an individual and respond to their physical strengths and learning style in full context and with care. And one of these few is the instructor you want.

## WINDS OF TRAIT

As a veteran teaching pro once sagely pointed out, "To err is human. To really screw things up requires an instructor." So here are some more considerations to mix into the desirable-or-not-instructor decision mix.

A skilled tennis teacher is not a dictator. Or a drill instructor. Or a grouchy junior high vice principal. Or a potential date. Or a nattering scold. Or an egomaniac. A skilled instructor is a guide. *Your* guide. A professional instructor is also not on their cell phone or checking their calls or texts, or talking to other students who pass by the courts during your lesson. You paid for their time and their attention. When you are on the court with that person, you are their only student.

So, what should you be doing on that teaching court?

You should be working with your crack teacher, who is dressed professionally and focused only on you, on forming a balanced tennis game. One with definite strengths and no liabilities. And one that edges along the continuum from where you started to where you want to end up steadily week after week.

At least that's how we hope it goes.

Occasionally, however, before you can go continuum surfing, you have to first smooth out the undertow.

Or as my golf pro friend, Zach, says, "If you need to spend fifty lessons focusing on squaring the clubface, then spend fifty lessons squaring the clubface." So it goes with tennis. If you have a lingering stroke issue from your past, you may need to spend a chunk of your time in the present clearing it up. If that is your situation, correct the problem with whatever amount of time that takes and then move on. Good priming makes for good painting.

However, if all systems are go, go, go, and your instructor persists in only teaching you groundstrokes, but ignores volleys and mid-court shots, and serve, and serve return, and overheads, then you need to find somebody who can consider and instruct tennis in all its dimensions. And show you how to develop that multi-dimensional game.

Because a determined opponent won't offer you only one kind of shot. Or only the shots you want to hit. They will find out the shots you don't have or don't like and make you keep hitting them. That's what they're taught by the real instructors to do.

And one more thing here.

Don't apologize for or take care of your instructor's bad moods. If you have to write off an unproductive session (that you paid for) to, "Oh, you know, he (she) was just in a bad mood today," then find someone else.

You see, here's the scoop – if you're being paid to hit tennis balls all day for a living, you don't get to have a bad day. You just don't. A professional behaves professionally. And part of that professional behavior is not bringing their personal baggage onto the teaching court.

If an instructor can't stay in a positive mood receiving your money to play tennis with you, he or she has a problem. Give that instructor the proverbial Nike to the hindquarters. He or she is no professional.

So, bottom-darn-line, make sure your instructor is of steady disposition and good cheer and is teaching you all the shots. At their best, tennis instructors are a valuable repository of knowledge about the full range of strokes. So, make them teach them all to you. Not right away, of course. But, not never, either.

And by the way, the obligation for your improvement doesn't only go one way.

## WHAT BECOMES A LESSON MOST

What you learn depends equally on you, the student. So –

Don't be a complacent student.

It's easy to keep working on the strokes you like and ignoring the ones you don't like. But it won't make you better. Don't allow yourself to settle in to just grinding week after week on the same two or three strokes. Challenge yourself. Make yourself be inquisitive and sometimes uncomfortable as you improve your game. The best students request every ounce of their instructor's knowledge. Because smart, involved students know that –

Some instructors know about much more than strokes.

Ideally, a competent, complete instructor is not only your guide, but also your resource. Make him or her prove to you how much she or he knows about all facets of the game. Ask a lot of questions. Think about your game. And challenge your instructor to think about *your* game as well. Ask for advice and counsel on diet, stretching, pre-match warm-up routines, tips for focus, tips for nervousness, and strategy advice, and see what information you get.

Your instructor may not know the answers to all of your questions in every area, but he or she may be able to point you to the answers that they don't know. Plus, think of it this way as well. No student was ever given less attention by a qualified, engaged teacher for themselves showing interest, initiative, and engagement, were they?

Instructors can be valuable hitting partners and playing partners as well. Their steady predictable pace can help you build your tempo and consistency. They can also simulate different types of opponents in practice points, so you can prepare your strokes and strategy for what you may see from the variety of playing styles you'll encounter in tournament or league tennis. In fact, for some advanced players, this may be an instructor's most valuable function. That, and the ability to not change any strokes that are already working just fine thank you very much.

And good instructors can give you knowledgeable feedback about matches that they have watched you play or that you have described to them. All of the abilities instructors have can help you get ready to develop and hone your match technique.

### TRUST BELT

And a little more about you and your part in all of this.

Your improved tennis game begins with seeking, securing, and receiving quality instruction. And to be truly successful as a student, a player, and possibly as a human being, you need to trust. Yourself. Your instructor. And, eventually, your game.

Your improved tennis also demands a willingness to be uncomfortable and fail. And while I don't subscribe to the mindless pseudo depth of that popular cliché, "You learn more from failing than from succeeding," failure is part of the betterment of skills landscape. Get used to it and get over it. You can't improve unless you find your weaknesses and correct them. That said, you still learn more from success. Like how to succeed again. Nobody needs to learn how to fail more.

Your improved tennis also requires the maturity to celebrate the successes and to know how to bring your self-image into present time. It takes integrity and honesty to admit to yourself at least that you're as good as you are, and not forever the player you were in some previous incarnation. And that may be the highest hurdle of all for game development. So, you up for all that? Of course you are. You bought a dadgum tennis instructional book.

So, discuss your progress and your goals with your instructor.

Develop a plan to realize those goals. And be prepared to modify your goals as you, like, totally improve. Know that tennis, like many high skill activities – martial arts, piano, violin, stand-up comedy – requires technique and practice. As with piano, tennis deftitude is best acquired by practicing often. Fifteen minutes on each of five days will cement skills better that one 75-minute weekly practice, or one once-a-month practice for five hours.

You need constant contact with the game to develop sport fluency. Part of the reason is that tennis strokes are not just about the mechanics of those strokes (which are certainly difficult enough), but also very much about the many micro-adjustments needed to get your body into the best position to hit those strokes. Contact with the sport and attentive practice trains your eyes to watch for subtle differences in bounce produced by differences in your opponent's string-bed contact, racquet-head-speed and angle, and the clothes worn by that person. There's a lot going on on the court that needs to be seen repeatedly so your brain can download into memory the many different ways a shot will reach you. And these saved files need to be opened often so the adjustments will become habitual.

It has been pointed out by many other sports theorists – some with impressive degrees, others with equally impressive self-appraisals – that the conscious brain hinders our motor skills and interferes with the smooth workings of tasks we know how to do. Tennis technique needs to be automatic and subconscious. You can't will tennis into submission. You can't force high-skill activities. They have to work their way into your body. It doesn't matter how great you were at basketball, lacrosse, or duck pin bowling, those sports are not tennis.

Tennis is tennis.

It is not intuitive. It is not natural. And being good at it has just about zero relation to how fast you can run or how high you can jump. So check those expectations at the entrance gate and get ready to suppli-cate yourself to the mighty gods of physics, mechanics, and repetition. Tennis will humble you and lift you up, but only if you take in what it is and what it has to offer humbly, rigorously, and attentively.

And find yourself a good instructor.

### *ADDITIONAL INFORMATION PRESENTED AS A BONUS IN ORDER TO INCREASE PERCEIVED BOOK VALUE –*

Tennis is not soccer, or baseball, or basketball. (But you knew that.) Our chosen ball sport is not like other ball sports, and in one specific way.

In sports without hitting implements, where it's just you and the ball, you move across the playing field and line up *your body* with the ball to strike it or catch it. Do this in tennis and you end up with a very cramped shot. In tennis, when you move across the court to chase down a shot, remember, you need to position yourself so that *your racquet* is lined up with the ball – not the old bod-o-rama. Give the ball some space on your hitting side. It will make your swing freer and more powerful.

## 2

# FINDING DEMO

*"You can't fall off the floor."*
Paul Vierra

So, now that you've gone out and secured better instruction, what else could you possibly need?

Well, a game-winning, door-slamming, killarr racquet, of course.

The racquet you play with is as important to your success on the court as a pen is to a writer, or a brush to a painter, or an ACME rocket to the Coyote. And it affects your self-image as a player. While it's true that no racquet can make you better, it's equally true that a bad racquet can make you worse. And look worse.

And you don't want to be worse. Or look worse. Do you? You want to be better. And look better, too. Right?

And you want to inflict you some The FOING, don't you? Of course you do.

So, the next gap to fill in your quest for more consistent, successful match play (and more of the aforementioned The FOING), right after sound, repeatable technique, is a racquet that complements your playing style and ability. A racquet that will allow you to use every good thing you have learned from your knowledgeable, professional instructor. A racquet that works with you, and not against you. So, right now, get a grip, don't give yourself too much time to think, and ask yourself –

Is your racquet holding you back?

## MATCH STICKS

You may not show your age (and in fact, if I may say, you look great), but your racquet does. If you bought your current manual ball-hitting device back in the dim days before the iPhone, molecular gastronomy, and the Las Vegas Golden Knights, then you should think about trading in your old friend for a newer friend. Because that friend you're counting on for wins on the court may not be as steadfast a friend as it was in 2003. And, if you're really honest about it, it was probably 1997 or so when you actually bought it, wasn't it?

Yeah, okay, you might say, what if I did by it in '94? What's the big deal? It still works. It isn't broken.

Well, as in many other areas, racquet 'technology' has advanced some. And the advances could help your game. Racquets for sale right now are lighter, bigger, and made of stronger, lower vibration material than they were over a decade (or two) ago, in that distant, mid-tech past. But I'm well aware that material improvements alone are not enough of an argument to convince some contented or stalled players to switch sticks.

Many players like the racquet that they're playing with – the racquet that they're used to. Sure, today's racquets may be technically better, they'll admit, but, the thinking goes, isn't a tennis racquet still just an implement with a woven stringbed that you hold by a grip and hope to use to hit the tennis ball to the other side of the net on the tennis court? Isn't it just that simple? Huh?

Well, yes. And maybe.

And, therefore, consequently, goes that line of thought, who needs a new one?

Well, you, probably.

Think of it this way – what if that (estimating generously here) fifteen-year-old trusted ball-whacking implement is standing in the way, even a little bit in the way, of your winning more matches? And opening a big ol' can of The FOING on your opponent. What then?

As simple as a tennis racquet is, *in concept,* small differences in feel, power, spin, weight, and balance can have big effects on your game – and how often you beat that suspiciously tall woman on that nasty public court USTA team who dresses like she's just auditioned for *Flashdance.*

But why is that? What changes over time with a tennis racquet?

Stress, my friends. Stress.

All materials have stress cycles – an amount of times the material can be called on to perform and still perform as it is supposed to. After about 400 hours of playing time, most racquets are substantially played out. That is to say, their liveliness isn't so lively no more. And they just don't give you their designed-in power- and control-creating resilience when they have been used for those hundreds of hours. You may not notice it. You may say that that your favorite racquet feels like it always has. But its decline is slow and subtle. Just as it occasionally is with our fellow citizens.

And, if I may say, since you're the one playing with the ever-less-responsive racquet, you're not the best judge of how well it's held up, anyway. You unconsciously re-adjust and re-calibrate your game to your racquet's reduced effectiveness every time you play with it. You adapt your strokes to its diminished effectiveness. After all, what else would a good friend do for a trusted implement? But that recalibrating and readjusting make it difficult to objectively evaluate your racquet. This isn't a criticism. It's a fact. And, yet, it doesn't make you the most accurate critic.

And consider this –

If you could rally with a brand new version of the same racquet you're using now, you would see what I'm describing immediately. I'm not kidding. You really would. Really. And don't give me the, "I'm not good enough to tell" business. If you're reading this book and you have functional hands and a working nervous system, you can tell.

The bottom line is this: If your racquet has gone dead, it is compelling you to swing harder for power, which can distort your stroke, and oblige you to make stroke corrections in the interest of accuracy that also compromise your stroke. Distorted, compromised strokes are not the path to winning tennis. Or The FOING.

## SLAM NUMBER EIGHTEEN

But a more accurate version of what you are capable of doing is not the only reason to consider the old upgrade-a-roo. Some players actually need more oompah-pah on their strokes. Are you maybe one of them? Roger Federer is.

El Fed switched from his beloved Wilson Pro Staff 90 to the seven square-inch larger Pro Staff 97 and suddenly found the ability to hit over his backhand more. And to slice less and hit harder. And beat Nadal. In a Grand Slam final. All of which helped reset and re-energize his already GOAT career at age thirty-four. You might benefit, too.

I have had students whose stroke mechanics had taken them as far as they could go. They hit the ball cleanly and effectively but have trouble increasing their serve or groundstroke pace to hit more winners or even to unleash more effective set-up shots. And while very few players finish a match they've just lost and think, 'I wish I'd hit the ball harder,' for a small number of players, simply hitting the same shot, or shots, with more ball speed would make a positive difference in their ability to play more successful and satisfying match tennis.

That's one additional angle on the why-should-I-replace-my-racquet question. Here's another. Perhaps your game has changed. Maybe your mechanics have improved or your stroke has lengthened. Or you've added more spin. Or you're hitting more accurately in the stringbed and your game is more powerful.

Or, again, maybe you truly do need to hit just a little harder.

These are some of the reasons for getting a new racquet. One other is –

can you hit the ball more effectively with some other racquet than with the one you're using now? If the answer is yes, you need to obtain that racquet. Right?

Many players wait to make sure that one or more of the good and legitimate reasons for obtaining a new racquet are satisfied before venturing to try something new. But, it's been fifteen years (or so)! What about trying something new today? Simply in the interest of the no-stone-unturned school of commitment to a worthwhile goal?

But where do you go to try one? And what do you do when you're there?

## SHOWROOM MODELS

You could repair to your local tennis specialty retailer – if there is still one around you – and simply purchase the stick that Fed or Rafa or Novak or Serena or Caro or your teaching pro is using, or one that looks good on the racquet wall, or one that the seventeen-year-old part-timer at the stringing machine with the untied shoes likes and take your chances. That could work. Or, you could try out a selection of strung racquets and make a choice that way.

This is called demoing.

The word 'to demo' is from the Latin verb, demonstare. Or from the American verb, to help you inflict you some The FOING. But you knew that.

If you do decide to demo, which is the preferred way to find an appropriate stick for your tennis match success, you will be playing with strung versions of the racquets you have under consideration and trying to determine which one fits your game the best.

If you do demo (and I hope you do), here are some things to remember –

Tell the shop denizens what type of game you have and what you're looking for and then let them recommend five or six possibilities. More is too many. Less is not enough. Five or six is just right.

Factor into the equation the length of your swing, irrespective of your ability. If you have a short swing, try at least one or two oversized (110 square-inch or larger head size) racquets. If you have a medium swing length, try mid-sized (95 to 97 square-inch head size) and mid-plus racquets (100 to 105 square-inch head size). And, if you sport a long, traditional swing, try a mid-sized (90 to 97 square-inch) racquet.

Why?

Because large-headed racquets naturally create more shot depth than smaller ones. And while hitting the ball deep trumps most every other tactic on the tennis court, hitting the ball out is always unproductive. A short-swinging player will benefit from the enhanced shot depth of a larger-faced racquet, while a long swinging player will fight the ball's tendency to fly long with this same racquet.

## TEST DRIVE

Take the five or six recommended demos out to a court at one time on one day, with a hitting partner or your pro aiding you in your test, and hit with them.

Really? All of them in one day?

Yes. It's difficult to remember the demo frame you used five weeks or five days ago in comparison to the one you're using today. And as with wine tasting, it's easiest and most productive to identify and compare different characteristics when you try all the candidates you're inter-ested in in one session.

But, how to do it?

After warming up with the racquet you use now, hit groundstrokes, volleys, serves, returns, overheads, and any other stroke in your arsenal with the demo racquets.

Try them quickly. Get quick impressions of the frames you're testing. And start weeding out the duds immediately. Because, there will be duds. And that's fine. Duds are good. Duds are our friend.

In fact, after all your diligent work in selecting a rasher of racquets to try, the best thing that can happen when you're demoing is that of the six racquets you brought to the court, you find that three of them spike the dud-o-meter and are out of the running right away. And the best way to find this out is to get fast impressions and once you've settled on a couple desirables, spend time hitting a variety of strokes with each of them.

Then, don't deliberate until next year's Wimbledon. Buy a new racquet. Soon.

How soon, exactly? One more demo session and maybe one or two more hitting sessions will probably do ya. And whatever new racquet you decide on through this process will be better than whatever you were playing with before.

And, just so we're clear, I'll say it again – Good equipment will not make you better, but bad equipment can make you worse.

An old, played-out racquet is forcing you to overhit and under-direct. And be less effective in vanquishing tennis foes than you could be. Don't be that player. Please. You were the one who said you wanted to win more matches. And, by extension, inflict you some The FOING.

Well, just a reminder, as was said earlier, this is gap-that-needs-filling number two to get you there.

## MORE DIRECTION

But back, for a moment, to that follow-up demo session.

The most helpful questions to ask yourself about a prospective new racquet are – Can I feel what the ball is doing off the stringbed when I hit it? And can I control the ball with this racquet? Control wins games, and feel helps with control. Any racquet can be strung to play more powerfully. And it's easy to hit the ball harder by just buying a larger racquet. But what really matters in matches is: Are the balls you are hitting landing in your opponent's court, in areas where you want them to land?

You can sense the general characteristics of a racquet when demoing, but what takes more time is to feel how to adjust a shot or vary a shot with a new and different tool. A racquet may only fully reveal itself to you as you play some hours with it and let it talk. Much of tennis is the adjustments made in a swing when the ball makes contact with the strings. And there is really no way to know how a different frame will respond in all circumstances until you've used it for a while. That's why a second, focused demo session is important. Play points and feel what the racquet does when you have to adjust and make a point.

Then buy one.

The racquet is the most important piece of equipment in tennis. Get the right one. Get it right and play better. And inflict you some more The FOING.

## GETTING ALL PSYCHOLOGICAL

Like working on good form, if you are serious about winning more (and I'm going to assume you are, because, again, if I may point out, you bought and are reading this book), you need to improve all the parts of your game that are standing in the way of your success. So, if you're really serious about getting better at match play, you need to take care of the equipment question. Now. It's important.

Don't give yourself an easy out. Don't give yourself an excuse for failure. Don't be one of those people who plays the poor-unworthy-me game. 'I don't deserve some fancy new racquet.' 'My game isn't good enough.' You're good enough for proper equipment whatever level you are. And, just so you know, proper equipment is actually more necessary for lower level players than experts anyway. Just don't make it easy on yourself and give with bogus excuses for losing.

To be more specific, and more general (and, yes, to be a little badgering as well) –

Don't say you want to do one thing, but act in some ways like you don't believe you really do want to. In tennis or in life. No matter how unconsciously you do it, don't excuse it. Don't fall prey to it. Put everything into your game. Don't leave any detail unexamined. Play hard. And if you win, you win. If you lose, you lose.

There is no shame in losing, especially if you've tried as hard as you can, and taken every step to win. But there's nothing good in pretending you're trying to get better at something, let's say, for instance, tennis match play, but leave yourself a sneaky unacknowledged little out so you'll have an excuse to console yourself with it if you don't succeed to your standards. Right? So, what's the answer?

Don't do it.

Exactly.

Plan to win. And use every resource to make it happen. Get a new racquet. Fill that second gap. Experience you some The FOING.

Because the next gap is waiting to be filled.


### *ADDITIONAL INFORMATION PRESENTED AS A BONUS IN ORDER TO INCREASE PERCEIVED BOOK VALUE –*

The numero uno simple, easy, inexpensive equipment tip for instant game improvement: Change your grip. Often.

If it's an overwrap, change it every time you play. Think: Kleenex. Use it and discard it.

If it's a full-on replacement grip, change it every thirty hours. For the clearest visual indication of yup-it's-time-to-change-the-thing, use a white grip. When it looks like fifty percent or more of its surface has been airbrushed with poi, affix a new one.

Your grip is the vital connection between you and your racquet. It needs to be a firm and positive connection that you can hold with light pressure. A slippery grip makes you squeeze too hard and impairs your muscular elasticity, your strokes, and your The FOING potential.

# 3

# FIT FOR COURT

*"I don't jog. If I die, I want to be sick."*
Abe Lemons

Tennis is a violently asymmetrical game. If you do it right.

So is your body ready to do it?

Tennis puts high demands on one side of the upper body – the hitting side. While the other side – the non-hitting side – though equally important, gets much less of a workout. In the process, tennis unbalances your muscles, jars your joints, and tests your tendons.

Furthermore, tennis is an aerobic sport *and* an anaerobic sport. You need to start quickly. And stop quickly. And you need to start and stop repeatedly over the course of several hours. And if you can't do those things repeatedly *and* effectively, you can't expect to use your game to repeatedly and effectively beat opponents. And if you can't do that, how can you administer you some The FOING?

All of which brings us to the third gap in your game – your fitness.

However fit you are for any other sport or activity, the question for your tennis game is – are you fit enough for tennis? Fit enough to drive back ten or twelve running shots and not be so winded after winning that point that you lose the next three? Fit enough to play a hard match in the morning and play hard again in the afternoon? Or the next day? And fit enough to place a violent, asymmetrical load on your muscles, start fast and stop hard, chase down balls over the course of a few hours, again and again, and still finish the match with enough energy left over to lift a beer and eat a pizza?

Are you fit enough to do that? Because, if you are, you can win tennis matches. But it's not as easy as hitting the treadmill twice a month. Tennis fitness is a particular kind of fitness.

You may look sublimely ripped in the mirror at the gym. You may do Pilates and yoga and Zumba. You may spin three days a week. But can you play the type of baseline or net game that you want to play and *need* to play in order to win, and keep it strong for a couple of hours? Are you really, truly, pinky-swear fit enough for court? I only ask because I've seen many a fine athlete take the match court expecting to triumph, and then get worn down and worn out by the sport, with games still left to play for the win.

Now maybe I'm wrong and your personal fitness checks off all the necessary strength and endurance boxes, and you can go the distance with your strokes no matter what the distance is. And you do look sublimely ripped in the mirror in the gym. You do Pilates and yoga and Zumba. You spin three days a week.

If so, get thee another green smoothie, skip ahead to the next chapter, and get to work on filling some other unfilled gap. You have my in-print admiration and respect already. And it's only the third chapter. So, congratulations! And right darn on!

If, however, your fitness doesn't check every box, or at least not as many of the fitness boxes as you would like, you can still partake of a green smoothie and read on. I think this will help.

For those of you with the fitness box waiting to be checked, we'll begin with a question – Where in the body does true tennis fitness start?

## LOOK OUT BELOW

What is obvious to anyone who has ever watched or played tennis, is that the arm swings the racquet. (And to think, you bought a book to find that out.) So arm strength looks important. And, in its way, it is. And yet, when we look at the world's best tennis players, their arms and upper bodies are slender relative to their lower bodies.

What does this mean?

Are they just training wrong? Are they ill-suited for the sport they dominate? Or do they or their trainers know something we don't?

Well, this much is certain: Every sport molds the athletes' bodies who participate in it to that sport. So, when most of the athletes in a certain sport exhibit the same types of muscular development, it's because the sport engages and strengthens those muscle groups.

Every sport also typically *attracts* athletes with certain body types to it

– many times simply because it's more natural or easier for certain types of individuals to play a certain sport. (Think: really tall humans playing basketball. Really thin humans running marathons. Humans with few teeth playing hockey.)

Now, how about tennis?

Tennis strokes are powered predominately by the large muscles in the lower body, and that's why tennis players are typically more developed muscularly from the waist down than from the waist up. Rafael Nadal's impressively large Los 'Guns' look great on TV, but Señor Nadal is, in fact, generating most of his substantial spin and power from his tree-trunkesque legs and is, to a certain extent, just carrying around useless biceps weight. But he's an exception. Very few pros have big beach-worthy biceps. And it's because they don't really need them. On the court, anyway.

But back to the main point.

Because of the bending involved in getting below the ball to hit groundstrokes and volleys, and because of the leg drive needed to produce force in a serve motion, and because of the previously mentioned premium on stopping and starting, it is the muscles of the lower body – specifically the gluts, hamstrings, and quadriceps – that are the most important tennis muscles.

And that's not the only reason tennis players are more developed down-market. There are also net clearance and back health to be considered.

Ideally, you want to call on larger muscle groups instead of smaller muscle groups to perform tennis tasks. Instead of bending at the waist when you need to get below grade to hit a forehand, and asking the small muscles of your lower back to help you, you want to keep your torso upright – what one of my students has called 'Buddha Tennis' – and bend at the knees. Because once you bend at the waist, it's, like, more difficult to elevate the ball over the net, and more stressful on your back as well.

What this all implies for your match tennis prowess and preeminent The FOING application is that you need a strong and flexible lower body to play winning tennis. Big muscles take longer to tire and training these muscles to be stronger will help you play as hard as you need to for as long as you need to.

But how do you develop better lower-body strength?

The best way? The most fun way? Play a lot of tennis.

But if, unlike me, you have a life and don't have unlimited playing time and access to a court, there are some other ways to achieve more lower body might, as well.

What follows is a partial list of ways to improve your lower body and your upper body tennis brawn. If you can and want to do all of the exercises suggested, then by all means, order a deluxe and have at it. But as with the total amount of gaps you are choosing to fill, there's a lot to do if you do it all. So what's most important is that you do *something*.

Necessary Disclaimer #1: And, of course, remember to check with your doctor before you begin any new exercise routine, especially if you have specific health concerns or have had any injuries that could be affected by the new weight-bearing movements. But you knew that.

Necessary Disclaimer #2: Few specifics are given for most of the suggested exercises that follow because of long-ingrained tennis pro/author sloth and torpor and because instructions for these exercises are easy to find online.

**THE STRENGTH LOWDOWN**

**These are some useful exercises for lower body, big-muscle-group strength.**

- Wall sits. ('Air Chair.')
- Squats.
- Leg presses. (If you have access to an appropriate device.)

## CROSS TRAINING

**These are some useful exercises to improve footwork and build lower body strength and quick start speed.**

- Running hill repeats.
- Cycling.
- Soccer.
- Basketball.
- Ultimate Frisbee (Which is a fantastic cross-training activity and warm-up activity for tennis players, as well.)

And now, what about the aerobic part?

## BORN TO RUN

Despite its anaerobic demands, tennis is also an endurance sport. To vanquish foes, you need to be able to maintain energy and focus and not run out of gas, wind, or juice while you play and seek to apply The FOING.

And I hate to say it, because most players don't want to hear it, but running for twenty to thirty minutes three times a week is an efficient way to build that endurance. The running can be done outdoors or on a treadmill, and the cross-training suggestions above will certainly help supplement your running. But in order to develop endurance, there are few good alternatives to logging some distance on the road or in the gym.

And now, another in a long line of personal asides –

I was slow to warm up as a player. And while it probably isn't literally true, I felt like I never won a match in two sets. In those distant pre-saber-metrics days, I convinced myself that either I would lose in two sets or win in three. And it is probably true that most of my five or so significant wins as a player were in long three-setters. So, then, therefore, whatever the actual, statistical truth of the matter was, I needed my endurance to be formidable for all three sets if I was planning to win. And since I hated to lose, I was always planning to win.

Nonetheless, my perspective on match tennis was that, even though I didn't want to and wasn't planning to lose, it was fully possible that I might. But, my thinking went, I just wanted it to be impossible that I lost because I ran out of energy. Whatever the virtues of my game, I wanted to have them available for as long as the match took.

So, when I was a young sapling of twelve, I began a distance running program. And, to this day, I still run on pavement five days a week. I don't suggest that this amount of running is necessary for your tennis improvement. But, who knows, maybe you'll begin running and end up liking it as much as I do. Maybe. The main thing is that you do some distance running or distance-running-equivalent, especially if you too are slow to warm up on the match court.

And here are some more good reasons to goose that personal endurance quotient –

Tired players lose their legs and thereby their serves (among other things), just as tired basketball players lose their legs and thereby their jump shot. And running out of energy has other more subtle effects on your non-physical effectiveness, as well. If you get tired, your mental outlook dims, you become less optimistic and positive, and you make mental errors.

So, are your legs good for a whole match? For as long as it may last?

Does your wind hold up? Does your mind stay clear and positive? Are you fit for court? And can you get to the ball as fast as you need to? If the answers are 'yes,' you are probably already running or cross-training. If the answers are 'no,' consider, just consider, running and some of this as well –

### EXPLOSIVE FIRST STEP

The tennis court is not a large area to defend – *unless you start late to the ball*. Therefore, your first step to the ball is the most important one. Raw speed isn't a necessity in tennis, but quickness is.

**Here are a few suggestions (from the many possibilities available) on exercises that will improve your first step.**

- Run Lines – Starting off the court on one side, place on the court, in a line, a ball on the doubles sideline, the singles sideline, the center line, the other singles sideline, and the other doubles sideline. Then, starting at a position just off the court and behind the line of balls, pick up the first ball and bring it back and drop it off court where you started. Then go out and get the next ball and do the same thing. Then, one by one, pick up the other three. All five balls should now be off the court near where you started. Now, one by one, put them all back.

- Cone Weaves – In a lesson, or with a very patient and understanding and indulgent and accurate hitting partner who has a hopper of balls next to him or her at the net, place two cones about six feet apart about a foot behind the baseline. Start between the two cones at the center of the baseline. Have the pro or saint-like partner feed a ball to your forehand a few feet outside the forehand cone. Move to the ball, set up, and hit it. Then recover *behind* the forehand cone and weave *in front of* the backhand cone for the ball being fed to a position outside that cone. Recover again behind the cone. You will end up creating a figure eight pattern, always moving in front of the cone to hit and behind it to recover.

- Interval work – Go to a track. (I know, I know. But it can actually be fun.) Run three slow laps at a just above walking pace. Then stretch your hamstrings and quads lightly. Then run half a lap at 60–70% of your fastest pace. Then slowly (just above walking pace), jog the second half of the lap. Repeat four to six times and then run another three laps very slowly as a warm down. Then stretch.

- Le Preparation – Lay out your running or workout clothes and shoes and socks and towel in a place you can find them *the night before* your morning workout. (You *are* going to work out in the morning, aren't you?) Make it as easy and thoughtless and fast as possible to begin. Before you talk yourself out of it.

## RUNNING ON YOUR STOMACH

Of course, you don't want a weak upper body, either. Tennis is powered principally by the lower body, but better upper body strength, especially greater core strength, never held back any player. And always looks great at the pool.

Specifically, you want to sport strong *accelerator* muscles: the abdominals, shoulders, triceps, and biceps. And for muscle balance, increased swing speed, better posture, and injury prevention, you should also develop the *decelerator* muscles: the lats, posterior deltoids, trapezius, and rotator cuff.

Upper body strengthening needs to be done thoughtfully, however. The muscles of your upper body not only need to be strengthened, they also need to be stretched.

Tennis is a sport played by moving and inclining towards our opponent. Players of every level spend most of their time on court in flexion – the position of the body bending forward. Since our bodies are excellent adaptors, our muscles respond and mold to the positions they're habitually put into. This is called *adaptive shortening*. And, unmonitored, it can lead to a particular tennis look – lean and agile, but with shoulders pinched forward and the head and neck giraffing in.

You see, tennis treats our muscles much the same as when we sit all day at a computer screen or drive a car for hours at a time. It shortens the accelerator muscles in the front of our bodies and lengthens the decelerator muscles in back and can lead to rounded shoulders, poor posture, and back problems.

But we can fight back.

The muscle health formula is – if a muscle is too tight, lengthen it, and if a muscle is too weak, strengthen it. Yoga poses that put your body in extension – that is exercises that put the natural curve back in your back – can undo the postural ravages of our violent asymmetrical obsession. Beyond that, be conscious of your posture. Work to keep your shoulders back and a curve in your lower back.

Here are some upper body exercises that will engage both the accelerators and the decelerators –

## HARD CORE

- Sit ups.
- Crunches.
- Planks.

## CURLS FOR THE GIRLS (AND BOYS)

- Curls.

## CHEST FOR ALL THE REST

- Pushups.
- Dips.
- Pull-ups.

## SPEAKING OF SAPLINGS

And then there's flexibility.

- Stretch *dynamically* before you play. What does that mean? It means movement is the best pre-exercise means of preparing your personal body. Here's one sequence you can do at the court –

- Jog at a very slow pace four times around the court. Do exaggerated, slow hurdlers strides across the court. Windmill your arms five times in each direction. Cross your chest with your arms ten times. Swing your racquet in air groundstrokes and air serve motions ten times for each. Using the weight of a strung racquet is a very effective upper-body stretch.

- Stretch *statically* after you play.

- Go to whatever your favorite stretches are for hamstrings and quads, shoulders and forearms.

## DRINK UP

- Try cherry juice before you play to prevent cramping.
- Drink water early in the match and stay hydrated on changeovers or every fifteen minutes.
- Drink low fat chocolate milk after you play to help with recovery.

And –

## BEYOND STRENGTH

- Lose weight.

Recommending this is like recommending running. No one generally wants to hear it suggested, because it's hard, demanding, and not fun. But even the loss of a few pounds can make a difference. Elite tennis players tend to be slender *within their body type.*

And it makes sense why.

The less weight you're carrying around, the easier the pounding of the game is on your knees and joints. The less weight you're carrying around, the stronger your back will be. And the less weight you're carrying around, the less weight you're carrying around. You'll use less energy to accomplish the same tasks and have more oompah-pah to hit the ball harder for longer.

## ZZZ WORD

To make it all work best, get enough sleep.

Lack of sleep affects mood, vision, coordination, and focus. Not to mention that lack of sleep arrests muscular repair after exertion and slows recovery from injury. Many top players strive to get nine to ten hours sleep per night. Try to get eight. Don't check your email again. Shut off the TV. Forgo that last glass of wine – no matter how good the vintage is – and go to bed.

## LAST WORDS

Again, and for the last time in this chapter, you don't have to do all of what has been suggested in order to improve your strength and, more importantly, your endurance for match play. Do whatever you can and have time to do to fill in the fitness gaps in your game. Because the results may cascade. Once you do something and see some results, you may just want to do more. Just, please, don't lose an otherwise winnable match because you ran out of energy. Okay?

Just get a little more fit. For court.

### ADDITIONAL INFORMATION PRESENTED AS A BONUS IN ORDER TO INCREASE PERCEIVED BOOK VALUE –

Studies have shown (and it may be true as well) that when you concentrate on the muscle group you're exercising, that group responds more positively to the training.

A study of a group housecleaners who believed they needed to exercise more, measured their strength and endurance and flexibility to establish a baseline. After the initial measurements were made, they were told (with supporting data) that their daily work was actually the equivalent of getting ripped and golden in specific ways in a gym. Tested weeks later, with no change in their regimen except a new outlook, all their fitness measures improved.

Visualize the range of motion and the contraction and exertion of the muscle groups of your own personal body you are working on. Your training will be more effective when done this way rather than done wishing you weren't or thinking of something else. Focus and intention matter. The link is what you think.

# 4

## THINK GLOBALLY, HIT LOCALLY

*"I have exactly as much rhythm as you think I have."*
– John Oliver

So far we've been tightening up the nuts and bolts of everyday tennis – strokes, equipment, and fitness. And if you've filled all or some of those gaps, you're almost ready to return to the match court and get some hard-won data on how much you've helped yourself with the off-court improvements you've made. Before you do, though, I want to ask you a seemingly non-tennis tennis question –

How do you organize your experience?

And by that I mean this – Do you see the big picture and overlook the details? Or, do you focus on the small things and miss the larger canvas? In short, are you a forest type or a trees type? Well, here's the news about match play. Whatever your tendencies are, winning tennis players need to be able to exist in both worlds – concept and execution, match and point, global and local.

Before you retake the match court and test the strength of your newly filled game gaps, it's important to ask yourself what type of player you are. Because you see, dear reader, dear player, dear future The FOING inflictor, you need to find your game. You need to find it physically and mentally.

But what does that even mean?

## YOU'VE GOT RHYTHM

It is my belief that every player has a personal, internal stroke tempo – a speed of stroking that provides that player with the optimal blend of power, consistency, photographability, and The FOING potential.

More specifically, every player has a stroke pace at which he or she is hitting the chosen shot as hard as the situation and their game will allow *and* still landing it in the court seventy percent or more of the time.

So, the first step to finding your game (the big picture) is finding your internal stroke tempo (the leetle picture).

Your ideal speed may be harder than you're hitting now, or it may be softer. One thing is for sure; even if you do want to hit the ball harder, it's not entirely about racquet head speed. In fact, the only speed that we're really functionally concerned with is *ball speed*. Who cares how fast you can swing? This isn't Major League Baseball. We're trying to keep the ball in the park. As some pro once said, "Don't swing harder, hit it harder!" Many top-level pros and collegiate players swing at 75 – 80% to stay relaxed and increase their percentages. Swing speed is often over-valued, ball pace never is.

And so, therefore –

*What really ensures solid tennis shots at any speed is how many strings meet how much ball when.*

But what exactly does that mean in practice?

Just this.

Stellar, gasp-inducing sphere velocity is often created most effectively by solid, slightly-above-center-of-the-stringbed contact, not necessarily by a fast-moving racquet; and certainly not if that fast-moving racquet is consistently contacting the ball outside the most resilient part of the string bed.

Or, more simply –

The best way to achieve reliably solid contact is to swing the racquet at a speed that, *for your strokes*, allows the most strings to meet the most ball most effectively the most often. In other words, optimal personal swing speed leads to better contact and more power with lower effort. All good and desirable stroke attributes.

So how do you find this ideal swing speed, this internal tempo, this game-defining rhythm?

Practice. Look. Listen. But, most of all, practice. As one famous oil painting instructor once said to a class of students, "Y'all don't paint enough!" Same for tennis players. Y'all need to practice.

But not match practice. Not quite yet. I know you want to get out and play some games and sets, and we will. Soon. But first here are two suggestions for finding your stroking rhythm on the practice court –

- Hit with your pro. Don't play points. Don't make it competitive. Just rally the ball back and forth from the baseline and find the most comfortable tempo that allows you significant ball speed and seventy percent or more in-the-court consistency. Have rallies where you count the number of shots in your exchanges. *Feel* the stroke when it achieves your natural tempo. *Remember* the feeling, so you can return to it in a match.

- Hit with a consistent, steady hitting partner. Don't play points. Don't make it competitive. Just rally the ball back and forth from the old baseline and find your most comfortable tempo.

That's it. Sort of.

It may take a number of sessions to lock in on your tempo, but keep at it. And realize that this personal tempo thing can be flaky and fleeting at first. Because even after you find and feel the right personal rhythm for your strokes, that sublime, low-effort optimal tempo can get all distracted and run out on you for no discernable reason in a match. And sometimes, if you play a match against a player with no rhythm in their game who is hitting inconsistent shots at you, it can just up and leave you. So like anything else we care for, our personal stroke tempo needs to be nurtured, protected, and minded.

And if, for no reason, or some reason, your tempo gets all whacked out and takes a walkabout, go back to your pro or your consistent, steady hitting partner and find that tempo again. Speak nicely to it. Think positive thoughts about it. Be understanding and accepting. Don't force it to come back to you. You are reprogramming ingrained hitting impulses that may be causing you to hit too hard or too daintily, and you need to gently, and with compassion, remind your body of its newly-discovered natural tempo.

Identifying your personal stroke rhythm is one of the most important small-scale steps you can take in building a more successful match game. After you find your preferred tempo, you can use it in your match warm-ups to establish your game for that match, and you can go back to it if your game starts to derail during the match.

### NUMBING SAMENESS

Once you've found your personal stroke tempo, it's time to pair it with a steady, dedicated, unwavering commitment to NUMBING SAMENESS.

What does *that* mean? It sounds like you're suggesting the mindless hitting of an automaton. Or Mats Wilander.

I am. But in this way –

Numbing Sameness means that your stroke rhythm and your *stroke execution* both be as close as possible to the same *in every stroke*. It means that if you watch a video of your strokes in a match, and pull out any section at random, your strokes should look the same as they do in any other section taken out at random.

Your set up, your back swing, your swing, your weight transfer, your follow-through and your racquet face angle should always be – you guessed it – the same. The incoming shot doesn't throw off your stroke. The tension of the match doesn't throw off your stroke. The score or the situation doesn't throw off your stroke.

Your strokes are numbingly the same. Every time.

Tennis, like knife throwing and reading the nuclear launch codes, is not an activity that you can do approximately right. Your technique needs to be the same every time – both your swing mechanics and your rhythm. It needs to be numbingly the same.

## THE IRRESISTIBLE BUT ODDBALL FORCE

But what if I can't always be numb and the same? What about people who hit at me really hard? Or really soft? Or just really weird?

As my quotable golf pro friend, Zach, said, "There are only two types of players – those who play for money, and those who don't." Ditto for tennis. If you're not a pro, you don't *have to* play anyone you don't want to. So if you can control the selection of opponents you face, do. As a general rule for happier tennis and a happier life through tennis – play up. Play the best players you can. Always. Your game will be better for it.

However –

If you are a tournament player and can't avoid playing the rhythmi-cally challenged undesirables of the tennis world, stick with your personal numbing sameness – in your technique, and in your stroke rhythm. And, like, don't veer from it. And, for the love of all that is holy in tennis, don't improvise. Please. Don't try to make up some new, never before seen stroke for a difficult testing situation in a match. Just hit the stroke you've worked so hard to craft and make the best of it.

How's that again?

Right. So, in case it wasn't totally clear before, here it is again – *no matter what kind of shot is hit at you, stick with your stroke*. Against the fast hitters, you will need to get your racquet back sooner. But other than that, play the game you want to play, at least in the area of stroke speed.

A tough truth about tennis is that you need to take the high ground and hit technically sound strokes when your opponent isn't, or can't. If you don't, their irregular input will fry your circuits and tilt you like a teen.

So, stay with your game. Your happiness and your budding relationship with The FOING depend on it.

## YOU'VE GOT GAME

Not only does every player have a natural rhythm, but I believe that every player also has a natural playing *style*. You may be aggressive and offensive or more cautious and defensive or an opportunist.

You need to find out where you fall on the scale of playing types.

I have written about these playing styles in my first book, *Occam's Racquet*, so I won't rehash the ideas presented in that book here. (Thankfully and conveniently though, *Occam's Racquet* is available in three formats on Amazon.) However, it is important to make a decision about what kind of player you are and what kind of player you would like to be. It will determine what strokes you work on in lessons, what strokes you practice, and, most importantly, it will determine what type of strategy you take into your matches.

## YOU'VE GOT A PLAN

Speaking of…

Every player at every level who plays matches and wants to be successful in matches and apply The FOING, must have a *plan*. As former Stanford men's tennis coach, John Whitlinger, once said to one of his players, "When you walk on the court, I want you to have a plan. I don't even care what plan it is. Just have one." Can I get a 'yeah?'

Even if your strokes are not fully developed or not yet developed as much as you'd like them to be, you still need a plan. Not having one is a big gap in your match game. You need to decide, based on what type of player you have self-identified as, what types of strokes you will be focusing on in your matches. For instance, if you are a defense-minded backcourt groundstroker, you will probably want to engage in long, high-probability rallies and wait for the other player to make mistakes.

And if, for instance, there is a short ball, and you move forward to play it, you will probably retreat right after to the baseline. Because this is what a defensive-minded player is comfortable doing. If this is you, devise and stay with a plan that supports this style of play. Don't rush the net on short balls. Don't try to hit scorching winners from the base-line. Play the game you are comfortable with and win or lose with it.

Or, in other words, if you are the consistency-seeking baseliner described above, don't suddenly, for no reason, begin trying to crush groundies, or hit lobs, or work on some manic-spin dropshot you've never really practiced. Impromptu stroke invention is no recipe for in-match success.

It might be fun to watch Gael Monfils or Jo Tsonga fool around and experiment in a Grand Slam match and think, "What an inspired artist he is," but the 'crazy player' gambit rarely confuses an opponent in the light-of-day world of actual match play. It usually puzzles them for a few moments, right before they get a broad, goofy grin and realize you have no idea what you're doing.

As the old saying goes, "Dance with the game you brung."

And it's still good advice. But that doesn't mean you have to keep using the game you brung *in the same way* throughout a match you're losing. You may have also heard this even older saying: "Never change a winning strategy, always change a losing one." In other words, carry on with the plan, but have a back-up plan that may not be as comfortable as the preferred plan, but may be necessary to go to if things start to go all jiggy.

## YOU'VE GOT A DREAM

We've been in the stroke trees, but as we ascend ever higher above the game-game forest, take a broad look at how you like to play and ask your tennis self what your vision of your game is. Baseline? Serve and Volley? All-Court? Or maybe some personal hybrid of the three? Whatever kind of game it is, you need to see yourself doing it and see yourself keeping on doing it, even if at first you don't seem to be succeeding with doing it.

So, some advice.

When you play a match, don't judge how well your game and your plan are working too quickly. Let your game warm up. Let it settle in. Give the plan a chance.

It's not easy to know when the strategy, *your* strategy, needs to be changed, but this much is certain – that time isn't during the first or second game, or the warm up, or before you've given it a chance.

And even if, later in the match, you've regretfully resigned yourself to changing the losing strategy, never change what you've been doing just because you can't figure out what else to do. If you are at that point, especially early in a match, it means that you haven't come prepared. Prepare to play the way you want to play. A way that respects your stroke rhythm. And a way that respects your plan.

## YOU'VE GOT TACTICS

And, finally, plan on what shots or combinations of shots you will use to create the winners that will help make your plan successful. Of course, not every ball is an opportunity for a point-ending shot, but some are.

For instance, let's say you serve wide to a right-hander in the ad court. The opponent's return of your serve will typically float predictably back up the center of your side of the court, at a convenient, step-in-and-whack-the-ball, two-thirds depth. The returner is also conveniently left recovering, on the left half of their court, while you are in the middle of yours. The shot combination here is simple – move inside the baseline, and return their return with a crosscourt forehand to their forehand corner for an easy winner.

This is just one classic example of a shot mixture you can use when it presents itself, or one you can engineer with serve placement and follow-up. But it illustrates how shot combinations help you win points. (And, providentially, there is another chapter devoted to this idea as well.) Have two or three likely combinations in mind when you arrive at the court for a match, ready to use or ready to be created when possible.

Practice points with your pro and hitting partner are excellent times to explore the combinations that work best for you.

Know what your shot combinations are. Recognize them. Create them. Exploit them. Visualize them before you play. Intend on using them when you play.

And, in general, know what you're about on the court, physically and mentally, overall and in detail.

Think globally. Hit locally.

### ADDITIONAL INFORMATION PRESENTED AS A BONUS IN ORDER TO INCREASE PERCEIVED BOOK VALUE –

You can't usually win a point with one shot, but you can lose it with one shot.

Though many players act like they'll never be given another chance, you don't need to win the rally on the return of serve or the return of the return. If the opportunity is juicy and offered up, take it and be glad. But it's perfectly fine and often advisable to follow up a serve or a return with a solid maintenance shot. Then let the rally develop. Let the opponent make some mistakes. Let the point come to you. Don't beat yourself. Make the opponent beat you. It's more challenging for them that way.

You want to put your opponent in a state of emergency. You never want to put yourself in one.

# 5

# FREE YOUR MINDSET

*"I know kung fu."*
Neo, *The Matrix*

Before you hit the match court, with your improved form, your state-of-the-science equipment and fitness, and your game plan in hand and in place, there's one more gap to fill. Your attitude.

In a high-skill sport like tennis, attitude may not be everything, but it's not nothing, either. Like strokes, strategy, and movement, it is something. And it's up to you to determine if it's something positive or something negative.

An improved attitude may not land you a down-the line topspin backhand, an ATP-level serve return, or a courtesy car and appearance money, but it will determine how you learn, how long you keep learning, how you practice, how you compete, and how you progress. Or, in short, much of what really matters for match tennis success. If your mind gets in the way of your body, your attitude isn't working for you. For success on the tennis court, you need to free your mindset. But first you need to know what your mindset is.

## FIXED FOR GROWTH

The idea of a mindset, in the sense I'm appropriating it here, comes from Dr. Carol Dweck's slyly-titled 2006 book, *Mindset,* and it's a valuable seventh tool in any player's six-pack bag. Like a fast recovery step, a fresh string job, or a triple-digit serve, your mind is often the difference between winning, losing, or fully grasping Hegel. In other words, how we view the world and ourselves affects our success.

In her book, Dr. Dweck says that we condition our view of the world by looking at it through one of two different lenses – The Fixed Mindset or The Growth Mindset. And this bi-focal worldview has big implications for tennis players. The good news is that a mindset, like a mind, can be changed.

Dr. Dweck writes that people with a Fixed Mindset believe in an unalterable, luck-of-the-draw, providence-of-birth kind of natural talent. In this view, geniuses are simply born geniuses, the gifted unalterably the gifted, and all the exceptional performers and performances we see in any area of life or sports are so because of the native talent of the performers. According to this view, if I am not in this group, I am doomed to mediocrity and probably a lower seeding, if I am not in this group. And maybe, more significantly, if I am one of the chosen talents, then I am destined to be exceptional because of my innate gifts.

By contrast, those individuals in the Growth Mindset group look at talent as open-ended, improvable, and always evolving. For them, learning is a joy, failure is a challenge to be embraced, and struggle and uncertainty and discomfort are the necessary components of improvement. And not just in sixth grade, junior prom, or building IKEA bookcases, either.

Improvement is open to all who will work for it in all areas of life, from the trivial to their tennis game. In the Growth Mindset worldview, greatness may begin with great physical or mental gifts, but it matures and takes hold because of a lot of darn hard work. Robb Strandlund and Jack Tempchin may have said it best in their song for the Eagles "Already Gone" –

> So often times it happens that we live our lives in chains
> And we never even know we have the key

Indeed.

As Glenn Frey sung back in 1974, a Fixed Mindset can be paralyzing and destructive for humans and especially tennis players. But the Fixed Mindset, like bad line calls, eight-and-unders grunting on drop-shots, and lack of turn signal use, is prevalent. "Fixers" may resist trying to improve or may avoid playing opponents they think they "should" beat if it means chancing failure. They may have extraordinary natural talent, but don't take it very far or quit when they start losing or encounter difficult new skills. Fixers believe that their natural talent should be great enough to guarantee their success and that having to practice to improve shows that they really aren't as gifted or as smart as they have been told. They can feel betrayed by the talent those around them have always lauded them for.

In short, they have problems.

In sharp contrast, the Growth Mindset can be liberating and empower-ing, and belongs to the players who practice well, improve, succeed, and banish self-doubt like a sitter overhead. "Growers" are "already gone." They take every opportunity to test and improve their skills, no matter how long it takes, or how it looks, or how it feels when they do. When they come up against a challenging stroke or match situation, they resolve to figure it out. They persevere, knowing that a skill like tennis takes tenacious, dedicated practice no matter how big your quadriceps are. They don't let their own walls hem them in.

Of course, we mustn't be categorical or silly or categorically silly. The world is not black or white. (Although, some shots are clearly in and certain lycra items should never be allowed in public.) And rarely is any person or tennis player completely one or the other mindset. Everyone is a blend, but seldom a 50-50 blend. One of these two mind-sets controls you and it's important to your improvement and well-being that you know which one does. And here's one way to find out.

## NATURAL TENNIS PLAYERS AND OTHER FIXER JARGON

You often hear a talented player described as a "natural," even on HD TV, by announcers paid to be prompted better by their producers. But is there such a thing as a natural tennis player? Or, is it simply the fixed mindset at work at the court and in the broadcast booth?

I've met and taught and coached many fine athletes who excelled in other sports disciplines, and many of them became very skilled tennis players, but in thirty-six years of teaching tennis to every level player, I can honestly say that I've never met a "natural" tennis player.

This is because tennis is an *unnatural* sport. Many of the most impor-tant parts of strokes (the serve toss, for instance) or full strokes (the backhand comes to mind here) are dependent on mastery of motions we don't use much at all anywhere else in our everyday lives or even in most other sports.

And this is good news for tennis players at all levels who want to improve their strokes and their match game and apply them some The FOING.

Why?

Because tennis is a sport that is only partially dependent on native athleticism. It's not a fixed sport, it's a growth sport. Good engineering, an understanding of physics, and an interest in doing a motion correctly and repeating it correctly over and over, thousands of times are much more important than your forty time, your vertical leap, or how much you leg curl.

More than many other sports that depend on raw athleticism, tennis relies on *technique*. And technique, by its very nature, is *learned*. And *must* be learned. Nobody "naturally" perfects or even executes flawless technique. That's why it's *technique*. So even the best, most gifted athletes begin this sport at the same place as all the other kinds of athletes – *at the beginning*.

Everyone has to learn it.

Tennis is also an equal opportunity humbler. And an equal opportunity exalter. Not everyone can be a pro, but everyone can get good at tennis, if they practice enough and in the right ways. And, of course, you can always dress like a pro if you shop diligently. What does this mean for you as a player and as a student of the game?

It means that the players who seem like god-gifted, natural tennis players aren't, because *there is no such thing*. Burying the idea of the "natural" player can take you a long way toward general happiness and a rejecting of the Fixed Mindset. All fluid, skillful tennis practitioners have to work to perfect their beautiful, natural-looking game and so will you. And there will be awkwardness, uncertainty, and stumbles for them just as there will be for you. Just as there were and still are for Federer, Nadal, Williams, Mugaruza, and that sandbagger you played in USTA last week with the hundred mph kick serve who claimed she was a 4.0.

We all put our forehands on one follow-through at a time. We just sometimes make the mistake of seeing the astounding finished product and assume that tennis greatness is a divine gift and that this gift is immaculate, inviolate, unearned, and unearnable.

Perish the thought. Today. It isn't.

High-level tennis talent is earned through sweat, mistakes, disappoint-ments, and tenacity. And often lots of cash, since some instructors don't really like checks or any paper trail.

## AND SO WHAT ABOUT YOUR INSTRUCTOR?

In a way, this all takes us back to the first chapter.

The instructor you are going to trust with your game as you succeed, fail, gaffe, expose you ego, engage in self-doubt, and generally work through the learning process as you try to improve, needs to under-stand how all this works, too. This person needs to support you and guide you as you get better. And most importantly, your instructor needs to believe that you *can* get better.

As I made over-clear earlier, it doesn't matter how many pro matches an instructor has played, and it doesn't matter what academy or club or method they're representing. If they approach instructing with a Fixed Mindset, they are going to limit your progress and your happiness. Instructors can be as guilty as players of orienting themselves to their students with a fixed view of their potential.

You see it every time an instructor is impatient ("you should already know that"), critical ("no one with your skills would make that mistake"), or fatalistic ("I don't think you'll ever be better than a 3.5"). Really? They know that? If they're that good at predictions, get some stock picks, romantic advice, and lotto numbers from them while you're at it.

Like a safety razor, political opinions, or dramatic irony, a frame of reference like the Fixed Mindset can cut two ways. It can lead to both over-praise *and* over-blame. For students and for teachers. Parents, friends, and lovers may laud your natural ability, while some instructors may disparage you for your inability to transcend it.

Don't accept limitations in either direction. Don't accept the Fixed Mindset. Demand for yourself instruction that allows for unlimited growth without presuppositions about how far you can grow because of some alleged "natural" talent. And write them a check and leave a paper trail if you want to.

## PSYCHIATRIST, ANALYZE THYSELF

But, there's no need to worry. Even Fixers can grow.

If you've identified yourself as a Fixer, that's okay. You can change your mindset and improve your game. Now's the time to decide to become a Grower. If you have a problem learning new skills because of the discombobulation and anxiety inherent in the process, try to find small ways to challenge yourself, ways that won't be obvious to your practice partners and opponents. That way you can aim small and miss small and find out how to gradually learn big. Here are some suggestions for mild, endurable change. There are many others.

- Change the racquet face angle on your backhand.
- Adjust your finger position on your serve toss.
- Modify your footwork on approach shots.

Make a small change and see how it feels. And remember, it's all going to be okay. Despite the fact that you think everyone else on court is watching you and charting your progress, you are the only one who notices any dislocation in your game. Or cares. Your opponents and hitting partners are all watching their own strokes or shoes or the supermodel on court six, anyway.

And though you will be venturing out in a small way, the failures as you perfect a new micro-skill will be small also. In this way, you can accustom your ego to success and improvement coming out of trial, tribulation, and occasional failure and thereby give yourself permission and leeway to fail much bigger and learn much more in the future.

### REJECT THE PLATEAU

All of which brings us to a golf analogy and to the poster athlete for both the Fixed and Growth Mindsets (and a few other qualities not related to our current topic) – Mr. Tiger Woods. Tiger's phenomenal early- and mid-career improvement as well as some of his equally phenomenal public displays of poor ball-striking come because of his Growth side.

Throughout his varied career, he has consciously refused to stay on a plateau. He has realized that the plateau is comfortable, safe, and known. But a great Growth Mindset athlete doesn't want to stay there and risk becoming complacent and fearful. To grow into the Growth Mindset, it is important to recognize when you are on a comfortable, successful plateau and purposely challenge yourself to move off it and get better. Then, even when you don't get better, you keep your mental edge and reinforce your growth attitude.

But unlike the Growth Mindset side of Tiger, his Fixed Mindset side can lead him on some long, unprofitable journeys trying to find the perfect swing. The lesson here is that once you have a swing that can win the U.S. Open at Pebble Beach by fifteen strokes (or go to the District Finals with your 3.5 team), don't believe your talent is so great you can then do anything you dream up. Instead, focus on plateaus in other areas of your game and don't tinker with what is working. Otherwise, you may get stuck at fourteen majors. Or at number three doubles.

## HOW TO PRACTICE AND IMPROVE

These ideas will work for either mindset. They will jolt and prod the Fixer and challenge and delight the Grower –

- Change your practice routine. Tennis players can often behave like mow-blow-and-go gardeners. They get routine-bound and their games get paralyzed. They go to the practice court, do the same warm-up routine every time, practice the same strokes they already do well, neglect strokes that cause uncertainty or discomfort, and then complain that they're working hard and not getting better. Change is scary. Change is also good. And productive.
- Work on strokes that aren't comfortable or grooved. Take your weakest stroke and try to improve it.
- Then take your best stroke and try to improve it.
- Practice your strokes in a different order.
- Spend two weeks just working on your serve. Or volley. Or backhand overhead. Then spend four or six or eight more weeks on one or all of those strokes.
- Work on movement or a strategy that you have trouble with.

- Hit really hard.
- Hit really soft.
- Have a hundred-ball rally.
- Learn a new spin.
- Add the drop shot.
- Prepare yourself to be surprised in a match by surprising yourself in practice.

### HOW TO COMPETE

During a practice match every now and then, change your match tactics.

If you are a diehard baseline basher, try adding in a serve and volley point every now and then. Or, if you always try to close points early, prolong a rally on purpose and see if you can win a point on percentage or on defense. Not just to be different, but to astonish and confuse your opponent and keep yourself awake and stimulated.

On the one hand, this may seem like you're simply putting yourself in an uncomfortable and potentially embarrassing situation. On the other hand, it may be incredibly freeing if you remember that this is not your usual game and you therefore have no particular stakes in the outcome.

### READ THE BOOK

And read Dr. Dweck's book, *Mindset,* and learn more about the way this theory can improve your tennis.

### MOVIN' ON

As I said earlier and as you can now attest, there have been a range of suggestions put out there in these first five chapters about how to fill the gaps in your game and improve your performance on the match court. But this is only one third of the equation. We also need to look at what you're doing when you're actually playing, and what you want to do after you finish a match. But all in good time.

Before we leave the Foreplay section, I just want to remind you that the way to improvement and more victorious sets and matches and The FOING is to take whatever amount of the suggestions given so far that are compatible with your time and inclinations and use them. If you don't do anything, you have no right to complain about your losses. But if you do something, anything, no matter how small, you can complain all you want. But I'm hoping that the story will be different for you.

If you agree with yourself that you truly want to improve and not just say to yourself that you want to improve, then you will do something, maybe even some things, and you'll start to win more often.

Deal?

Okay, so now let's take this stuff to the court.

## ADDITIONAL INFORMATION PRESENTED AS A BONUS IN ORDER TO INCREASE PERCEIVED BOOK VALUE –

When you're winning, you not only play better, you get 'lucky' too. In fact, most Grand Slam tournaments are won with not only one walkover and a favorable draw, but also with some help from the tennis gods. But there's nothing too mystical about the gods and their plans for you. They reward engaged detachment. Aim for the outcome, but don't obsess about the outcome. Execute your shots and strategies and accumulate points and games, and the 'breaks' that help you win will come to you.

The breaks you get from being diligent but not controlling are like the sudden inspiration you receive after you've worked a problem hard, fall short of finding all the answers and then get biffed on the forehead by an insight when you get up and take a walk. Intend to win, be aware of the score, but let the flow of your game take you where it takes you. That's how winners get lucky.

# SECTION II

## PLAY

# 1

## WARM-UP PACT

*"In all matters, before beginning, a diligent preparation should be made."*
Marcus Tullius Cicero, *On Duties*

Okay, you've made strides with your off-court work and filled in some of the gaps in your game. Now it's a beautiful day, and you're excited about getting back out on the rectangle and playing a practice match. As I've mentioned, unlike me, you have a life outside of tennis and you don't get as much court time as you'd like to. So, naturally, you want to get to it.

Your opponent arrives, you pop open a couple cans of new balls, hit seventeen groundstrokes, and your opponent says, "Ready?" You nod agreeably, spin the stick, announce, "First good," and you're off.

Way off.

Already.

Like a band going full bore during the sound check, you started playing too soon.

A clever student calls what you and your opponent just did the *microwave warm-up*. You cook through the pre-match duties the fastest way possible so you can get to the meat of the matter – playing games and scoring points. But if you really want to win points, games, matches, and notch you some resounding The FOING, is the fastest way the best way? Or should you slow cook your warm up?

## THERE OUTTA BE A LAW

There's no rule that says you have to warm up. Of course, there's no rule that says you should be excellent, either. Or wear shoes. But players who want to succeed do all three.

But you don't have to.

Even the five minutes allotted at tournaments is a convention. There and everywhere else, you could refuse. You could choose not hit the ball to your opponent. You could sit on the bench and play "Fortnite" or check your Alibaba stock (by the time you read this, probably both outdated cultural references), but you should warm up. Why? Because if you don't, you won't be ready. Even the pros do it, though you'd hardly know it, since no one really discusses it.

In TV tennis, the warm-up gets no love at all. It's usually the time when the camera goes tight on the announcers, shoulder to shoulder in their little booth, as they set up the match, predict who's going to do what how, and run lists of player positives and negatives. But rarely do they talk about what the players are doing before the point scoring starts. And the camera usually only shows a few shots of the players' warm up. And why is this? Well, because, like much of the TV audience, the announcers don't care about it.

We all want to see tennis when it counts – points, games, sets, and matches.

We want to see the drama, the emotion, and most of all, the stakes. Tennis that matters. The warm-up is like rewritten pages, re-recorded albums, or soufflés rising on the tenth try. All necessary to perfect your craft, but ignored, overlooked, and cunningly concealed in the popular media narrative of innate excellence and instant proficiency. (See: the preceding chapter.)

But thoughtful practice and methodical pre-performance preparations form the unglamorous, but vital underbelly of our high-skill sport. And every other sport. And sushi.

### WHY WARM UP?

Is there really a case to be made *against* warming up?

I mean, come on, does any player at any level out there really believe that they will play as well without preparing as if they do? Is there any player who wouldn't want to take every legal advantage in order to play better? Of course not.

And, my friends, there are two good reasons why every player should warm up.

One is to prepare yourself physically and mentally to play your best. The second is to take advantage of this singular pre-match opportunity and use it as a tactical weapon.

First, the obvious stuff.

## THE OBVIOUS STUFF

Physically, the warm-up makes a difference. And it starts at home or wherever you are before you go to the court. It's in what you eat, when you eat, what you're thinking about, and, even, what the speed of your movements is. Rushing before a match can make you rush during a match. As Yoda might say, "Rush not, lose through unforced errors not."

And once you're at the court, with your mind in focus, it's time to prepare your body. Time to engage your dormant tennis muscles and remind them of what you're about to ask them to do. Time to prevent injury and promote efficient movement. Time to break a sweat, and literally make your body and muscles warmer. Time to make the physical transition from whatever you were doing before to playing tennis now. And time to show off that new shirt.

It is also time to get out all the random strokes that will be stroke errors in a match *before* the point counting starts. And it's a time to check in with your strokes and, as importantly, your personal stroke tempo. Every day on the court can be a new day, and often is. So, find out what your game has in store for you before you have to use that game for real.

The warm-up also provides time to make the mental transition from "regular" life to life on the tennis court and its specific needs, rules, etiquette, and ontology. Time to adjust your eyes to seeing a spherical object flying toward you. Time to engage your brain and focus on your current activity. Time to concentrate on your constructive distractions. Time to look up "ontology."

## THE SUBTLE STUFF

But maybe you're already committed to all of that. And regularly using the word, ontology. Good. Then you're ready to use the pre-match time on the court with your opponent to gain a tactical advantage. Our sport is unique in putting us in contact with our opponent with a chance to influence the outcome *before the competition starts.* How great is that?

So use this time to check out your opponent's game. Feed that person various strokes and various heights, spins, and speeds. See how the player you're going to compete against responds. Find a weakness or two. Mentally catalog some areas to attack once the match begins.

The warm-up is also a luscious opportunity to start controlling the match. How? By taking the early initiative. Instigate decisions. Take charge of who takes the balls from the tournament desk, which side you start the warm-up on, and who spins the racquet for serve and side.

It is time to set the tempo of the action on your terms. Signaling that you are the one in charge pays off later in a match and gives you a subtle, unseen psychological advantage throughout. And maybe better line calls.

*In short, the warm-up is a time to take time and gain a small advantage before you start.*

## HOW TO WARM UP

Get to the court early.

There is a difference between a tournament match and a casual match. You should always take time to fully prepare your game before a tournament match. You should do the same before a casual match, too, but there isn't always time.

**But if you do have time before a match –**

Coerce a hitting partner to meet you. Then drive, bike, walk, Uber, or have your driver take you to the court and direct your thoughts to tennis and *your* tennis game on the way.

Get to the court early enough to jog lightly for five minutes and then stretch your major muscle groups – shoulders, quads, hamstrings, and hips. Say hi to your hitting partner. Thank him or her for coming to help you. Accept compliments on your shirt. Then, starting slowly, hit short groundstrokes, then full-court groundstrokes, then volleys, then overheads, serves, and returns.

In preparation for your serve warm up, count in practice how many serves you need to hit to get on track for seventy percent or more serve consistency. For most players, it is at least forty to fifty practice serves. For some, fifty-one or even fifty-two. Whatever amount of serves it is, hit that many serves or more in your pre-warm-up warm-up, and then lock in on some returns, too.

How long should this take?

It varies by player. I needed 45 minutes to really rev my game up, but I was a slow warm-up. Some players can do it in fifteen minutes, and for them, spending more time just means expending more match energy. Experiment with this. Find out what *you* need. But, by all means, do it. Then, when the ceremonial five-minute match warm-up comes around, you can use that time as body and muscle re-loosening opportunity as well as time to assess and dragoon the opponent's game.

**If you don't have any time before a match –**

Perhaps because it is a casual match and time is short, or perhaps because you are at a tournament with limited practice court availability, there are times when there isn't really time for warming up before the official warm-up, that you aren't actually obligated to do. On these occasions, choose a few things that are critical to your game and make sure you work on them.

And on a tight schedule day, even your drive to the court is crucial to getting you ready. On the way there, think about your game. Envision shots you want to hit, hit the way you want to hit them. Review your shot combinations and your game plan. Make sure your outfit matches your shoes.

Then once you're there, make sure your body is as ready as possible to start playing effectively. If there isn't room or time to dynamically stretch, then just jog slowly in the parking lot or around the court. Do some practice serve motions and then some toss practice. Hit as many balls as you can before you start. Shame your playing partners into hitting longer and taking more practice serves than they usually do. Say you read it somewhere.

## THE WARM-UP IS NOT

And here's le big caution: The warm-up is *not* a time to work on strokes or try to change technique.

For the second and probably not the last time in this book – Dance with the game you brung.

The warm-up is not a time to outhit, outplace, or make it difficult for your opponent, either. You are engaged in a ritual unique to our sport – helping yourself *and* your opponent get ready for the contest. But if you cannot bring yourself to warm up in good faith and not excuse your lack of control or manners by virtue of your "competitiveness," it may be time to try a different sport. Maybe dodge ball. Or demolition derby. Play tennis. Play in the spirit of this mannered and mannerly game. But you knew that.

And by all means, make the most of all the hours and dollars you have spent practicing and taking lessons and filling the gaps in your game.

Spend some time before you play bringing your game up to speed, so that when the match starts, you are able to make the most of what you've practiced and learned and plotted and planned for. The pros, most of whom play more in a year than any of us will ever play in thirteen or fourteen months, would not start or even re-start a match without making sure they were ready to go. And these are trained, conditioned athletes with one purpose in their work lives: to absolutely maximize their income from ages 20 – 29. That, and to hit the ball the most effective way they can. So, okay, that's two tightly-related ideas, but you get the idea.

Don't also, please, my friends, judge pre-match how good the other player is by how they look or dress. Or even by the way that person hits the ball. You can't tell. You just can't tell. This may come as a shock, but players try to mask their ability – in their technique and in their get-ups. For experienced tournament hounds, this pattern of deception can start as far back as the juniors.

Many years ago, in the 10-and-unders, my son played a tall, physically mature boy with a powerful, schooled game who not only proceeded to wax him, but told him right before they started, "I'm only seven and this is my first match." (I think I heard he ended up in the Senate or prescribing opiates. Something like that.)

You just can't tell. But please don't be him. At any age. But, and, still, on the other hand, you don't want to show everything you've got in the warm-up, either. Impress the opponent by winning points. Take it slow and casual beforehand.

But you knew that.

To bring it all back to the purpose of this chapter – Doesn't it make sense to take every step to playing as well as possible? (That was totally rhetorical, by the way.) Anyway, here are some ideas on what steps to take –

## SOME WARM-UP TECHNIQUES

- Start the warm-up at home. Start the mental game there, too.
- Pretend you're playing for big money.
- Pretend your match is being broadcast internationally or at least watched by other people.
- Pretend you're on your own fantasy tennis team. (There's fantasy tennis?)
- Plan a warm-up session before any practice match or tournament match.
- Insist on warming up at the match court.
- Develop a timed warm-up routine and coerce someone into doing it with you. (Money may necessarily be involved.)
- Start all strokes slowly, concentrating on rhythm and form.
- Hit T to T first and then move back to hit full-court strokes.
- Warm up your arms and then your legs.
- Know how long it takes your personal body to be ready to hit match-worthy shots.
- Know how many bad serves you need to expel from your system to start hitting good serves for points at seventy percent effectiveness.
- Know how much time your body needs to get ready to play and win points.

- Know how much hitting time you need before the five-minute warm-up in a tournament.
- Know what you're going to do if there is not time to warm-up or if your opponent is rushing things along.
- Find ways to begin controlling the match in the warm-up.
- Know what to do if a goat rushes onto the court.
- Know what to do if a goat rushes onto the court with a nice one-handed backhand and a kick serve.
- Know the rules about drafting a goat onto your fantasy tennis team.
- Know when you're ready.

And, if you've done even some of that, you're ready.

Now you can play.

### *ADDITIONAL INFORMATION PRESENTED AS A BONUS IN ORDER TO INCREASE PERCEIVED BOOK VALUE –*

Warm up *slowly*. Hit your strokes half as fast as you will hit them in the match. Or slower. (The pros do. Your teaching pro probably does. Even Dave on your USTA team does. Sometimes.)

And make sure your warm-up is a double-decker. Or even a triple.

Concentrate on your upper body first – your swing and your racquet face position and your follow-through – and then check in with your lower body. You do want to move your feet, you do want to flex your knees, and you do want to transfer your weight, but you don't need to do it all at once. Then, check in with how well you're seeing the ball. Let yourself, you guessed it, warm up.

# 2

# FASCHING ADVICE

*"It's a hard thing to leave any deeply routine life, even if you hate it."*
John Steinbeck, *East of Eden*

Fasching is a German carnival and celebration. Started centuries ago as a way to blow off steam and mock the strict dudes in the castles, Fasching is a time for worry-free revelry. A time to let go of societal inhibitions and cultural strictures and carouse without consequence. Basically, college.

Fasching is a time to express inner passions, try something new, and feel free. Best of all, Fasching is like Vegas. What happens in Fasching, etc. Fasching is time out of mind. Fasching is exploration and experimentation. Fasching is wild. Fasching could also be very helpful for your improving match game.

## FASCHING MODEL

Fasching is often called the foolish season. But there is nothing foolish about finding a new way to renew your life. Or your tennis. At some point, everyone's game needs to get Fasching conscious.

No matter what level you play, it's easy to get stuck in a rut. In your strokes. In your strategy. In your weekly matches. You drill the same strokes you already own, avoid the ones you should work on to improve your game, and play it safe in your singles and doubles matches. We all like routine and routine is necessary for sports practice. And shaving. And nunchucks.

But routine can get routine and unthinking and uncritical and stifle progress. And with a high-skill sport like tennis, improvement is limitless, so why limit yourself to a safe way of playing? Step outside your comfort zone and get better. Especially since you've now dedicated yourself to improving your tennis match win percentage and a hearty embrace of getting you some measure of The FOING.

It's time for a Fasching makeover.

## FASCHING SCHOOL

This is how it works.

In your next practice session, take a stroke you do well and really push it. Tweak it. Play with it. Maybe blow it up. For one session anyway. Push it to the breaking point with more pace, or more spin, or some crazy angle. Don't worry about the results, just see how different you can make it. You may find something that you like and something you can use. A wicked sidespin forehand. A swinging topspin volley. A full-court backhand overhead.

Or take a stroke that you don't do well, or are developing, and use it in a practice match. Maybe it's a kick serve. Or a slice backhand. Or an all-out aggressive serve return. Dare to roll out that new, untested skill and see how it performs when you're trying to win some points. It's easy to think, "Oh, I just need to work on it a few more hours. Maybe some time I'll use it." But will you ever really try it? Or will you play it safe and just draw another well-worn arrow from the usual quiver? If the stroke seems solid in practice, you need to test it out when a result, even just a practice result, is on the line. If you don't, you won't know what it can and cannot do. And then how will you know when you can trust it in a match?

All of which leads in to some other classic tennis questions. When exactly is the right time to try out a new stroke? And how will you know? And how long will you wait? How long do any of us have to wait to try that new stroke? Carpe, as they say, diem. Just don't carpe an untested stroke in a match that counts. First, Fasching it to your liking and then use it.

That's the lower stress way to change your game.

We all need some time at the out-of-town tryout, or the Cactus League game, or the pre-grand soft opening. Not everything should hit the sports section. Not everything is for publication. In a society obsessed with prodigies and perfection, we need to understand that the dominant narrative is twaddle: improvement happens in steps. And out of sight. For us. For the pros. For everybody. Give yourself a chance to get better by temporarily getting worse. Hold a little personal Fasching.

And this bears repeating – *Don't worry about the results.*

Can you do that? Because, if you can, you can improve.

Spacewalk out of your pressurized game capsule and experience the weightlessness of your stroke and your game in a way you haven't before. In a daring and maybe dangerous way. In a way that makes you uncomfortable, but gets you to take a risk and maybe look dorky, but maybe allows you the freedom to find something you never knew you could do.

And before the inevitable self-judging Apollonian voice starts to whisper to you about how well or badly this Dionysian experiment is working, remember the rules – this practice doesn't count, misses don't mean anything, and you're just out on the court for some crazy time. Like a shot after the whistle. Like the PSAT. Like one of my fifty rough drafts. You can go back to safe tennis tomorrow.

Of course this disruptive (sorry about using that word) notion isn't limited to tennis. There are other areas where it might work as well – cooking, relationships, poetry. And some areas where it might not work as well – arms negotiation, driving, surgery, to name a few. So, you be the judge of how far to take it. And when to use it. But it's completely safe for use on the tennis court – as long as you can leave your ego at home and let the fixed mindset Mr. or Ms. Perfect voice go.

Can you do that?

## FASCHING DO'S

Weird, temporary strokes and strange spins used on the practice court are probably the easy part of our proposed romp-about. Changing *how* you play singles or doubles is much harder. But a good rousing strategy bacchanal can help with your game-game in this area, too.

Everyone involved just needs to know what the rules are and agree to them. In fact, you might even want a safe word, like "Miroslav Mecir" (outdated player reference) in case things get out of hand. In tennis or in poetry.

Let's consider your weekly doubles match.

This is the doubles match you play for grins and enjoyment with a couple friends and Lois from USTA. Everyone in the foursome knows that you all often end up in the deadly one-up, one-back formation, and you've all decided that you'd all like to come to the net more. You've discussed it, agreed to it, think it's a really good idea and, still, when match time arrives and there's a score involved, the receiver and server still keep hugging baseline.

Your doubles needs a change. A Fasching change.

In your Fasching session, you agree that that day *everyone* will approach the net on *every* serve and *every* serve return no matter what the consequences, until and unless one of the participants says, "Miroslav Mecir," and even then you might still keep doing it. *And you stick with the free-for-all pact for the whole session.*

Don't keep score. Don't worry how it looks. Don't worry how many you miss. Don't worry how weird it feels. In fact, if it doesn't feel weird, you're probably not stepping out enough. If it helps, wear a crazy hat or different clothes. Become someone else for the day. The whole idea is, for a little while anyway, to step out of and step out on the tidy tennis world you've constructed that may be holding you back. Live in another personality and return to the everyday with some secret you found at the carnival.

But you have to go with the Fasching spirit.

Let your game unravel a little. Let it get sloppy. Let yourself get loose to get better. Then, when it's all done, see if you liked it. See if you'll use the new stroke or strategy you tried. See what your friends thought. And have a laugh together. After.

## FASCHING ICON

Here's another idea.

Do a personal singles Fasching where you decide to play out of character in a practice one v. one match. Rush the net more. Clobber mid-court sitters. Hit forty drop shots. Hit thirty lobs. Approach on everything. Try to hit only backhands. Stand way inside the court on returns or rallies. Volley very close to the net. Or, from way back. Hit only first serves. Hit every ball like you're Dominic Thiem or Jack Sock. Just be sure to tell your singles practice partner what you're doing, otherwise, it can just look unstable. And Fognini's already doing that bit. And Safin's (second knowingly outdated player reference) retired.

But your Fasching practice doesn't have to be crazy.

Just experimental.

And different from what you do every day. After all, not everyone parties the same. Just take some time, in a way that's comfortable (or maybe even uncomfortable) in its uncomfortableness for you, to step out of your daily game and experience the court and your place on it in a new way. Joyously confront and throw over the Fixer in your sports psyche.

Fasching is like Mardi Gras – a time to stop caring and stop worrying. And re-find the fun in your sport. And this is le big idea: If you can practice worry-free, then maybe, just maybe, you can begin to play worry-free, too. Or, at least, worry-lite. Or, just a little looser. And maybe in the process, find the player you were always meant to be.

And discover a couple of new tools for the match kit and, of course, for the ever-desirable The FOING.

Here are some tips for your personal Fasching –

### FASCHING TIPS

- Pick a stroke or a strategy you want to improve.
- Pick a session to work on it.
- Let everyone know what you're doing.
- Choose a safe word.
- Warm up as usual.
- Remind everyone again of what you're doing.
- Go wild (or even semi-wild) and try something different.
- Remember, it doesn't count, it's Fasching.
- Remind everyone one more time of what you were just doing.
- Note what works and what you want to try again. (You can Fasching multiple times.)
- Go back to your everyday tennis with a sly smile, a new relaxed attitude, and a new skill or two.
- Repeat as necessary.

### *ADDITIONAL INFORMATION PRESENTED AS A BONUS IN ORDER TO INCREASE PERCEIVED BOOK VALUE –*

Performance goals set you up for failure. Outcome goals set you up for improvement.

When you're adding a new skill or trying a new strategy, don't ask yourself how well it worked, ask yourself, "How many times did I try it?" Putting pressure on that new kick serve that you're not quite confident of yet by worrying about how many times it landed in the box is a recipe for disappointment.

Instead, give yourself a specific and modest number of kick serves you want to hit that day (maybe five) and then find times when you're ahead in the count (40 – love or 40 – 15) and try one then. Next time out, try it 7 or 10 times. Success seen from this angle will simply be using it the amount of times you planned to, whatever the result. If you land them all in, so much the better.

# 3

# STAGE AND SCREEN

*"All the world's a screen."*
Some Stage Actor

I recently heard or read or imagined the following quote – "The difference between a stage actor and a screen actor is this: The stage actor reaches out to the audience. The screen actor lets the audience come to them." And, I might add, cashes an actual check for the work.

On a stage, the physical distance and diminished sightlines make it necessary to project what you're portraying in a bigger, bolder way than you would for the camera. But on screen, with so many variables removed and the camera intimately observing, the actor can, instead, just be present with what he or she is doing, and not project outward as forcefully. The audience will still get the message and the impact of the performance.

In fact, stage actors may have a difficult time knowing exactly how to convey just the right amount of performance when they are on screen. Just as some tennis players who've been told from the time they were innocent, susceptible groms to "be aggressive" can't help rushing their strokes on court.

The difference between the two approaches to acting is the difference between intrusively giving and consciously receiving. And on the tennis court, it's the difference between attacking mindlessly and adapting thoughtfully. And full control of The FOING.

## BETTER TO RECEIVE

So what's the answer? What are we supposed to do? How do we start? And what's the definition of The FOING again?

Good questions. To nudge your game onto the path of thoughtfulness and adaptation and therefore The FOING, just relax and remember –

Every great tennis shot is preceded by a pause.

Watch a professional on television or a skilled player at your club or court and you can see it. Before every shot there's a –

Pause.

An interval during which the player is ready, set up, and in position to commit shot, but doesn't commit it. A moment in which the player pauses in a coda of deliberate non-activity for a just a beat, gathering calm and composure right before making violent, powerful contact with the ball.

Without this reflective, intentional, stroke-composing interval, the shot can become rushed, contact compromised, shot quality scuppered, direction made unpredictable, and an unintentional pattern begun that carries through an entire match – the pattern of hurrying through the shot with the wrong tempo. And you know by now how important I believe proper tempo is for your game. And for The FOING.

So don't let rushing slow your tennis progress.

Instead, let the shot come to you.

Be a screen actor, not a stage actor.

It's true that players are often reminded to prepare early, move to the ball early, and go at and attack the ball. But as in the old fashioned, overused, ill-advised phrase, "rush the net," the fact of *attacking* the ball is not what the expression seems to suggest.

## THE QUICK TAN FOX

Many players I've worked with chide themselves for being "lazy" when they miss a shot, when they were, in point of actual fact, not lazy at all, but instead *overeager*.

In trying to make sure that they "attack" the ball and not let the shot get behind them, and take them out of rhythm or force them to hit off of their back foot, a player will overrun the shot, swing the racquet too early, make contact too soon, and see the ball end up either in the net or much farther crosscourt than they had intended.

Yes, siree, bobcat. I've seen it happen.

A properly hit stroke *does* include early racquet preparation, *does* include good extension, and *does* include the idea of going out and playing the shot, and not letting the shot play you. But a great stroke *must also include* that moment where you let the ball show itself to you – that moment where you clearly and calmly see the pace, spin, angle, and depth that you are dealing with before you dial up your response. What trips up many otherwise skillful players is that they don't take that moment and instead try to force the tempo. In the interest of not being too late, they end up being too early.

And there's even more here than meets the I. And the You. The idea of pausing, the idea of adapting, the idea of thoughtful play; all of those ideas are parts of an even bigger concept – Hit the shot you are hitting.

*Hit the shot you are hitting.*

Not the shot before it. And not the shot that may come after it. Hit the shot you are hitting *at the moment*. It sounds simple, but it's tricky. Actually doing it though can be the cure for rushing into shots and rushing out of them. And, conversely, not rushing into shots or rushing out of them can be the cure for thinking ahead or behind where you actually are. Think of it this way, is there a better method for being able to pause than making sure you're focusing on the moment?

Hit the shot you're hitting.

Every opponent wants to make you rush so you don't have time to set up and hit the ball the way you want to. We've all been in matches where it didn't seem possible to catch our breath or get ready quickly enough to react to the incoming onslaught. That's called distress, and it just ain't no good for winning tennis.

Some opponents may hit harder than we're used to or move us more than we're used to, but the answer is not to try to meet their aggressive tennis with even more aggressive tennis. That's exactly what they want. The answer is to slow the game down and –

Hit the shot you're hitting.

Don't let your own or anyone else's hurrying put you in a hurry. Don't also underestimate the effect of your opponent's personality or habits on your game – physically and psychologically. Assimilate what's happening and respond. Right after you pause and prepare.

### IF IT SOUNDS LIKE A FISH...

Here's a simple technique to correct the impulse to rush.

Wait

A

Darn

Moment.

Here's another, more specific way.

Say "wait" to yourself before each stroke you hit. Just the word, "wait."

If you take the time to say that one word and follow that one thought, you will have started construction on a path to a more relaxed, better-timed, more effective stroke. Just as when you move to a ball, you want to start early so you can be set and on balance before you hit, you also want to be composed mentally once you're set and on balance with enough time to say "wait" before you make contact. This way you'll know you aren't rushing the stroke and know you're allowing yourself to read the situation before you do the things.

One of the concepts of psychotherapy may be helpful in framing this idea in one other way. And it's this –

"Respond, don't react."

## JUNG AT HEART

Reacting can mean one of two things. Either, that you're allowing your emotions to overwhelm your judgment of a situation. Or, that you're not initiating the action and are only able to take steps that are hurried and ill thought out. Either sense of the word is a negative sense for your tennis.

So when you respond instead of simply reacting, you take in the situation, calmly judge the best course of action, and then choose what to do. Like a screen actor, you let the situation come to you. Like a tennis player who will improve their match game and repeatedly experience The FOING, you let the shot come to you.

Of course, you still have to prepare early, move your weight into the shot, and strike it cleanly, but you do it on your terms – in a relaxed, steady, and balanced way. You do not sell yourself like a stage actor and 'attack' your shots. Instead, like a great screen actor, you *wait* to take things as they come. You take what's given to you.

And you take control of your game.

Prepare, set up, and say "wait" before you hit. The transition to a smoother, more measured hit won't necessarily be easy or quick, but like founders shares, it will pay off in the future. Handsomely.

To sum up, my friends: Let the ball come to you. There you have it.

### ADDITIONAL INFORMATION PRESENTED AS A BONUS IN ORDER TO INCREASE PERCEIVED BOOK VALUE –

In June of 2018, Robin Soderling talked about his victory over Rafael Nadal at Roland Garros in 2009. He said that in order to beat Nadal, you have to play aggressively, and at the same time, be patient during some long rallies. He observed how hard this balance of focus and stroke selection is to maintain.

On a level the rest of the tennis population can relate to, know which shots are *maintenance shots* and which are *closing shots*. We're talking about context, observation, and patience, my friends. Your emphasis and intensity will vary point by point and sometimes within the point. Try shifting mental gears on the practice court to prepare. Or, if you have the chance, play Nadal.

# 4

## RACCIDENT COVERAGE

*"While in theory randomness is an intrinsic property, in practice, randomness is incomplete information."*
Nassim Nicholas Taleb

Have you recently been the victim of a raccident? You know, a short, off-the-frame squirmer that your opponent shanks uncontrollably into your near court, that then spins crazily and drops just out of reach for a lost point? Yours. The kind of unintentional winner that can bring match momentum and player equanimity to a crashing halt? If you think that you or a loved one or a doubles partner are at risk of a raccident, proper coverage can help.

## ASPHALT JUNGLE

You see, you just never know what's going to happen out there.

So you need to be prepared and protected.

Maybe you or a friend have witnessed something like this: You're in the midst of a hard, deep groundstroke rally and for no good reason, your opponent's response to your solid, well executed crosscourt backhand is a short, sidespin mishit to your ad court service square.

What the (if you'll pardon the expression) heck?

You can't exactly charge in, flail mightily, and smack this one back. It may sail long, losing you the point on a lusty overhit. Instead, you need to move forward quickly, set up solidly and early, bend your knees, and execute a backhand up the line to your opponent's forehand. Then reset for a volley and be ready to move across to your right to cut off and reach your opponent's follow up. If there is one.

But responding with that sequence of shots takes a level of deliberate action and care that the goofy shot your opponent birthed doesn't seem to demand. Ah, but unfortunately it does.

You see that's just one possibility of what you might encounter. And how you might handle it. But there are way too many others. Not-on-purpose drop shots. Low, spinning lobs. Mishit groundstrokes. Framed volleys. Mid-court floaters. Deep floaters. Wobbly half volleys. And, untold others where those came from – all of them limited only by your opponent's flawed or mis-developed stroke production.

And here's something else that's galling –

These annoying, damaging, ego-assaulting flailings are rarely done *on purpose*. Most of the time, the other driver of the ball doesn't mean to hit this junk and, indeed, probably wanted to hit something much better, but didn't. Or couldn't. But that still doesn't make you safer.

If you crash and burn trying to counter one of these shots, it's irritating, puzzling, and debilitating. You're not succumbing to superior stroking, superior power, or even superior strategy, but instead to dumb luck and trouble. It's easy to let yourself off the hook for not seeing calamity coming, and yet a point lost to chance and lack of skill is still a point lost.

## PLAYING UNDER THE INFLUENCE

So, when a raccident occurs, here's what you need to remember–

You didn't create this mess. You just happened to be in the way of it. It's not your fault and it's no reflection on you or how good your game is. *But you still need to return these shots effectively to make points* – especially at certain USTA league levels, or in the early rounds of some tournaments. Without the ability to protect yourself against reckless stroking, you can hit well, serve well, and return well and still have a difficult time winning sets and matches. And experiencing your deserved amount of The FOING.

A student once observed this about the game: Tennis is one of the only sports where *your* playing level can directly depend on *your opponent's level*.

Exactly. Good observation. I'm just glad he never decided to write a tennis book.

So, anyway, don't let a sudden drop in the opponent's level bring a well-played point to a sloppy end. Remember, it only takes a second. But the results can last the whole match. You need good coverage.

### HOW MUCH COVERAGE SHOULD I GET?

Get as much coverage as you can, and as early as you can.

How?

**Get to the scene early.** When your opponent chunks one over, don't wait until you've figured out exactly what bizarre, odd-vector highlight-reel squibber he or she has launched at you. That takes too much time. You'll have to figure it out on the way to the scene. If the opponent's ball is going to land short and crazy, you need to act. And quickly. But don't panic. Move to the ball early, set up, and then keep your feet light and move some more if you need to. And you'll often need to. It's easy to make these ad lib squib shots more difficult by setting up too early, and standing, unmoving, on the court. So get there as soon as you can, but keep your options open by chattering your feet in micro-steps and readjusting your court position as the ball's off-axis spin jerks it around and changes its position.

**Bend your knees and respect los flubbos.** Many flubs are flubbed back into the net or blown past the opposite baseline because they aren't taken seriously. Hitting these shots back can be more challenging than trading deep, searing crosscourt forehands or returning fast serves. And oh so much less enjoyable. So be patient, be intent, and respect each shot. These uncertain, squirrely framers take more concentration and respect than good, regular, official, instructor-approved strokes.

**Stroke the shot smoothly.** It's tempting to try to blast your way through those dinkers and weirdies, but more speed is rarely the answer. You cannot usually successfully add more than 50% to the incoming ball's pace on your return shot and still keep control of it. So, you can accelerate these shots some, but concentrate on placement and depth and a complete swing motion more than pace. This applies to shots picked up deep, too.

So, to review, for best coverage and protection –

Be Alert
Get There Early.
Bend Your Knees And Get Serious.
Keep Your Feet Light And Moving.
Set Up In Your Final Position.
Smooth The Shot.
Then, get ready for another one. And even if there isn't another one right away, you will still look strong, ready, and purposeful. And secure.

## LIMITS AND DEDUCTIBLES

The best way to practice safe and controlled set-ups is with matchplay. Lots of it. Against a variety of opponents. Find out how you respond to uncertain, unpredictable situations by putting yourself in them repeatedly.

However, since you can't always play matches, you can construct drills, too.

CORNER
Have your instructor or hitting partner feed one shot to your deep forehand corner and then one deep to your backhand corner and then cover whatever short, eccentric, or spinney shot they feed you for the third ball. And play the point out.

SWERVE

Start a rally and have your instructor or hitting partner randomly feed in sub-standard shots short or deep. Cover them and play them out.

MANUEVER
Stand in one specific area of the court and have your instructor or hitting partner feed you a range of the most creative junk they can concoct and smooth these shots back. This last drill also helps you when you're the one feeding junk shots. Because by creating them, you will be learning how and why they are the way they are and act the way they act.

## RE-FRAME JOB

Raccidents take a mental toll as well as a physical one. It can be a self-esteem-crushing bummer to lose to a player with ugly strokes that squirt and thrump around the rectangle and cause you grief and untold errors. You may begin to question your self-worth. You may begin to believe you have suddenly lost your game.

And all those things can happen, *if* you continue to try to use the game you usually play against a raccident-causing opponent. But as Steve Jobs famously said, "Think different."

How? What do you mean "different?" (And shouldn't it be 'differently?')

Just this: When is a winner not a winner? Answer: when you don't hit it anywhere near as hard as you usually do. Winners against an inconsistent player will cause you, if you plan to beat them, to reevaluate your concept of what a winning shot is. Since you can't smash back many of the no-pace, strange-spin, shanks and floinks you'll face out there for fear they'll be too much shot left at the end of the court, you must often rely on angles and open court shots to win points instead. These accommodation shots won't produce the adrenaline rush of a crushing forehand or a swinging volley against a solid player, but won't have the negative physical and psychological effects of losing against a hacker, either.

And so I ask you, which would you rather have? The big shot that goes out, or the medium-paced shot to the open court that makes the point and gets you the win? (I hope again that I'm being, like, totally rhetorical here.) In any case, triumphing over the raccident specialist is as much about re-characterizing what it means to hit winners as it is following the technical advice.

Still, the technical advice is important.

## DO YOU HAVE GOOD HANDS?

Learning how to properly execute volleys, half volleys, high volleys, low overheads, and off-spin bunt-backs will complete your portfolio of coverage. So, take some time off from the strokes you always want to practice and spend some time on the ones that will help you score in difficult times.

One way to be more alert and ready at all times on the court is to put some all-court elements into your own game, even if you're a diehard baseliner. The very act of purposely coming forward and playing a variety of shots in the forecourt puts you in a frame of mind to be ready to respond to shots at depths that you didn't plan for. It also improves your quickness and response in all areas of the court.

Good coverage and loss protection aren't flashy, but they win points, games, and matches. And contribute just as much to winning the matches you're supposed to win and to The FOING as the glitzy stoof. Watch a pro bout and notice that, even there, making the most of these strange, unintended gifts always helps. Even at high speeds.

So, please, if you want to get past the raccidents and proceed to the better encounters, cover yourself, plan for the unplanned, and, by all means, be careful out there.

### *ADDITIONAL INFORMATION PRESENTED AS A BONUS IN ORDER TO INCREASE PERCEIVED BOOK VALUE –*

Don't overlook good contact.

Master's champion Fred Couples was once asked how he corrects his golf swing on an off day. His answer? "I make contact one groove higher on the clubface." (And that's how I'm guessing you win at Augusta.)

Anyway, in tennis, when you want to hit any stroke more solidly and create more easy power, hit the ball in the *top third* of the stringbed. The center of the racquet face has long been referred to as the 'sweetspot', and it's not a bad location for ball-on-string encounters, but it's not the best location. On the predominantly oval or rectangular racquet heads currently in use, the area slightly above the center is actually much sweeter. Freddie would agree.

# 5

# TENSE STAKES

*"Tension is the great integrity."*
R. Buckminster Fuller

For as long as most any tennis player can remember, there's been some instructor or coach, or writer, or pundit who's told us to relax when we play. Relax our grip, relax our shoulders, relax our mind. Relax. Relax. Relax. It's enough to make Federer sweat. Well, almost.

But it's okay, they all had the best intentions.

Not completely accurate, but well-intentioned. You see, what they all counseled is a fine idea, it's just not the whole truth. Sometimes it's okay to be tense. Sometimes it's even desirable. That's right, tension can be good. Tension can be our friend. And tension can create stroke winners, if used at the right time in the right way for the right reason. But just how does that work? And when are those times?

Sit back, relax, and let's take a look.

### PRESENT TENSE

First of all, just to be clear, tension in sports *in general* is about as helpful as a 4.3 forty time. In chess. You don't want to carry tension around the court with you like some kind of high school pysch class project or Robert Bly duffle bag. It tires the small muscles that ultimately control racquet movement and hurts your stokes.

When you're in a ready position or in a point but away from the ball, you want to be barely holding the grip, balancing the weight of the racquet in your off hand, with your muscles basically at ease and engaged as little as possible. Straining to squeeze juice from your grip, hiking your shoulders like an '80s Kevin McHale, or baring your teeth like a mad hound when you're not even smacking the sphere just wastes energy and makes you look weird or like a lacrosse player. Even when you're off-court and not oscillating the orb, squeezing hard is not such a good idea.

Plus, as we all know, many beginners spend most of their energy on court gripping the racquet too hard. But though they overplay the idea, they're intuitively onto something many advanced players don't use enough.

## FUTURE TENSE

You see it's possible to overdo this whole "be loose for more power" business.

In the interest of staying relaxed, many players don't focus their muscle energy in the right amount at the right time. It's possible to be so loose and relaxed and light on the racquet that you force your arm to do the work your body should be doing.

All of which means you don't actually want to be at the same level of relaxation during contact with the ball as you are in a neutral or ready stance, or on a changeover. Exhibit number one is the forehand groundstroke. This is the biggest stroke in most players' bags and it needs the most focused, timed tension.

The moments right before contact are crucial.

Next time you line up to crush a big forehand, check in on which muscles engage right before the crushmeister is applied. Some are probably firing naturally, but which ones? For maximum power, your upper abdominals (yes, your eight- or ten-pack), hitting-side pectorals, and biceps should tense before and during the stroke to initiate the sequence of power moves.

But you're ready to engage them because you've read the relevant chapter and worked on these muscle groups, yes? Good.

And that's just the upper body. The formidable muscles of the lower body – your quads, hamstrings, and gluts, to name a few biggies – are performing similar pre-stroke loading and tensing.

And, again, you've worked on these muscle groups, too, yes? Very good.

Though it's the arm we see moving to hit the ball, the muscular drive comes from these three aforementioned upper body muscle groups in conjunction with the hitting-side shoulder and upper back. Contracting these big galoots at the proper time before impact instigates not only your swing, but your lower body drive and upper body rotation as well. And, almost as importantly, gives your arm support and protection.

Juan Martin del Potro may hang his arm out toward the back fence on his forehand back swing, and that works for him. He beat Federer at El Open. But, in general, allowing the arm to float away from your body on forehand or backhand groundstrokes invites tennis elbow and imprecise alignment and glancing contact with the ball. All undesirable. Without girding the three top-of-body muscle groups for impact and acceleration, you force your arm to do all the work. And, in tennis and in life, you want to make the big muscles carry the load, not the small ones.

These same muscular contractions are important for the forehand volley as well. The volley is a short stroke against a looming opponent and a ball not slowed down by court friction, and you need to brace yourself muscularly to prepare for impact and a successful redirecting of the ball.

To keep your contact solid and return the ball with the most power, using tension in the supporting muscles and squeezing the grip at the right time is the way to do it. Similar tension is needed for backhands, mid-court shots, serve returns, and sometimes handshakes. But you already knew that.

And just a reminder –

Tense, in the sense we're using it, means tightening the relevant muscles just enough to make the hit more solid. At the most, about 50% as tight as you can go. On a one-to-ten scale with one being almost letting go of the racquet and ten being steam rising from the grip, you want your serve to be a two, your groundstrokes to be a three or a four, and your volleys to be a five or a six.

Remember, it's tennis, not the North American Grip Strength Competition. Powerful muscle contraction without fluidity and flow is what those big guys with lots of ink, tank tops, and cargo shorts do at the high school courts. In a well-made stroke, the muscle group doing the most work during contact is the abdominals. Those eight to ten sculptured ripples aren't just camera fodder anymore, they should be leading the way to a ripping stroke.

## PAST TENSE

So then what?

Well, once you've hit the ball, it's time to relax it all again. No need to prime and stress your hitting muscles until the next time it's time to mash a winner to the open court. Done properly, what results is a repeating cycle of rest/tension/relaxation, with your grip pressure always the lightest you can manage, firming just a little when you're about to make contact.

Now, getting back to those beginners. Turns out they were onto something. While it's certainly true that you can tense too much and rob yourself of power, it's also true that you can relax too much at the wrong time and rob yourself of power. And precision. And, you guessed it, The FOING.

So tense smart.

We're not talking about Nancy Grace, all-the-time-for-no-good-reason tense. We're talking about a firm, helping push-start for a whole body stroke. Experiment with it, find the amount of tension that powers your strokes but doesn't shorten your swing, and use it when you hit the ball. Stay loose, stay relaxed, but know when to get tense, too. Just don't actually *be* tense and you'll be powerful. And so will your strokes.

### ADDITIONAL INFORMATION PRESENTED AS A BONUS IN ORDER TO INCREASE PERCEIVED BOOK VALUE –

In the ready position, the small amount of racquet weight that isn't being supported by your off hand should be felt by the forefinger and little finger of your racquet hand. There should be enough space between your racquet hand fingers and the grip that you can see a small gap.

Keeping the lightest touch on the grip when not hitting keeps your stroke muscles flexible and prolongs their match effectiveness. Use your energy for the important stuff – like actually hitting the ball. Or firmly shaking your opponent's hand.

# 6

## BACKHAND COMPLEMENT

*"A person is a pattern of behavior, of a larger awareness."*
Deepak Chopra

Every tennis game has patterns.

The pros have patterns. Look past their power and their personalities and you'll see them. (Their patterns, that is.) Recreational players have patterns, too. Look beyond the randomness and the errors and you'll see them at the public court or the league match.

Your tennis game has patterns as well. Simple ones – you hit every forehand crosscourt. Complex ones – you retreat in indecision after taking a mid-court ball; but not always.

You're probably not even aware of these patterns. They may seem like random events, or errors, or just the way you work the ball. But taken together, they show how you typically conduct a rally or close a point. Left unexamined, your patterns, like your mindset, may help you or hurt you.

And why do they matter?

Because if you don't choose your patterns, your opponent will choose them for you.

But where to begin?

## I CHING FOR ACTION

You can begin with this one simple but big idea: *All points have a structure.*

The structure might be chaotic, dependent on initial accidents of place-ment or power. Or, it can be orderly, put into the point according to a plan. If your pattern consists of hitting the ball back over and seeing what happens, and if you plan on winning more sets and more matches, you need to get more specific about your strategy. Today.

Because it isn't only points that have a structure.

All *matches* have a structure, too; the bigger plan that determines the tactics for each point. The question is: Who structures the structure in your matches? You? The opponent? The I-Ching?

All successful players at every level are able to do two things: 1) Impose their game on their opponent, and 2) Make it hard for their opponent to impose their game on them. And sometimes talk their way into free racquets or a couple of outfits.

So who are you, imposer or imposed? And what's your style when you do impose?

Maybe it's Andy Roddick, version 2003.0. You cash in with your big money shot whenever you get a chance and hope that'll do it. Or maybe it's pre-Gilbert Andre Agassi. You enjoy watching the other player run coast-to-coast in their backcourt, chasing down balls like a crazed arcade duck. But great offense in tennis for the rest of us is more than just hitting the ball hard or even hitting it hard corner to corner.

This kind of hit-and-sort approach obviously works best if you command mutant swing velocity à la Mr. Roddick or Mr. Agassi. But for the critical mass of the rest of the world's players, this isn't really a strategy, and not much of a pattern. At its best, it's a reflex or maybe a habit. At its not so best, it may even be a psychological condition – *tenniopathy* – a tennis-specific affliction that makes the game all about you and your strokes, but doesn't take the opponent and their game into account. And doesn't envision any tactic beyond simply landing the stroke on the other side of the net.

And remember this: Roddick eventually added a slice backhand to his two-shot arsenal to prolong some rallies and Agassi descended to 141 in the world before he found some ancient tennis wisdom pre-dating even the Open Era and increased prize money: *Great offense considers the whole court and both players.*

A properly righteous offensive game plan weaves together your analysis of the opponent, the tendencies of your game, and the prevailing court conditions, and tells you what will do the most damage to the opponent's game *that day*. It devises ways to keep the damage coming, whatever strokes that implies. This is the, if you will, conceptual chassis underneath strategic patterns, more wins, and, most desirably, increased The FOING.

## AN OPEN AND CLOSED COURT

At its most basic (or at least at its most clunky), effective tennis strategy has often been short-handedly described as *hitting it where they ain't*. And there are certainly matches where this is all the plan that's needed. You hit a serve, the return comes back, there's gaping open court across the net and you hit a ball there. Point over. The popular one-two combo platter. On days where that opportunity is repeatedly offered, seize it every time you can. And be glad.

But unfortunately, not every outing is a broad-side-of-the-barn gimme-fest. Against an opponent with some substantial skills, some moxie, and a well thought-out plan of their own, these yawning chasms of point-scoring glee may be few. And you may need a couple other ideas to draw on. Which brings us, finally, to the next important point –

*Sometimes you have to hit to the closed court.*

The *closed* court? What in the darn heck shoot does that mean?

What this means is – you put your opponent in a tactically tight space and watch the *forced errors* – the second best kind besides *unforced* errors – mount as that individual tries to fight his or her way out.

And closing the court starts with you, the player, developing or exploiting one good pattern.

More is too much. Less is just pound and pray. Clearly, unless you're Roddick or one of his tour descendants, you need something more than luck and a big forehand. But, by the same token, if you are mentally running through a range of strategic options during a match, you are just slowing yourself down and thinking too much on the court. As they say in baseball, "Thinking is stinking." Therefore, one pattern will do.

Take a moment right now and picture the pros. Do they think on the court? As little as possible. And the very best pros, do they even think *off* the court? About tennis, that is? Probably not, but their coaches do.

Since you may be between coaches at the moment, you have some pre-match thinking to do. And it's this. Choose a simple strategy *before* the match that's easy to remember *during* the match, and use it for the *whole* match. Take a page out of the pros' coaches' playbook – think when you're *outside* the court and just play tennis when you're *on* it.

### INTENT TO CONTRIBUTE

Tennis is a social network. (Sorry to use that cringer phrase but, you know, SEO beckons and it's almost appropriate here.)

Anyway, what I mean is that during a match, you and your opponent are connected and co-dependent for the outcome. What the other player *can* accomplish right now comes from the opportunities *you provide them*. And vice-versa. The shot you just hit determines the shot your opponent is hitting now. Even when serving, *your* patterns mold *their* game.

Not everyone has fully integrated this knowledge, however. Some players will work certain shot combinations for a while, and seeing no immediate payoff, abandon them and start in on some other combinations, allowing the opponent to escape way too easily. But how can you expect to desensitize the other player to your intentions if you don't intend them for long enough to be intentional?

You've got to make the plan, execute the plan, and stay with the plan. That's the plan truth.

Maybe this will help.

Here's a universal strategy and pattern sorter that works against every player regardless of ability: *Figure out what the other player doesn't want to do and make them do it repeatedly.* It sounds simple, maybe simplistic, but it's how to win. Many talented ball strikers lose by hitting repeatedly to their opponent's *strengths*. This is very polite. But you're looking for shots that taste good, not ones with good taste.

In a match, long rallies are sometimes, yes, a sign that two skilled opponents are engaged in a titanic battle. But more to our point, long rallies in a match are also a sign that no one controls the point. To win, you want the other player to net the yellow ball or hit it out *as soon as possible*. And in fact, *not* wanting to end points efficiently may be another tennis-specific psychological condition. But that's *way* beyond the scope of this book.

One great stroke doesn't make a great player (although Ivo Karlovic has enjoyed a pretty nice career), but hitting repeatedly to one location that hurts the other player strategically can make a great strategy.

## ONE OPPONENT. ONE STRATEGY. ONE TARGET.

The tennis you want to play is *Bludgeon Tennis: finding your opponent's weakest stroke and hitting to it at every opportunity*.

And when the opponent hits the ball back, attack this weak stroke again and again until it crumbles. For most players (including the most excellent Mr. Federer) this weak stroke is the *Backhand Groundstroke*. Work almost anyone's backhand over and over and you will win more points than they do. And thereby deliver unto yourself a large measure of The FOING.

If you need proof, consider these two Spanish words – Rafael Nadal. After all, where would Rafa be in the rivalry stats against The Federer (except for, maybe, in the last two years) without his relentless pounding of RF's high backhand? Exactly. Dictionaries define "bludgeon" this way: "to beat repeatedly with a heavy object," *or* "force or bully someone to do something," *or* "make one's way with brute force." I define it as "Rafa for the masses."

Be patient with your strategy. At least to a point. Like any good pummeling, it takes a while to tenderize the prey.

So keep at it even if it doesn't score points at first. Depth and placement are the cake of this tactic, pace and spin are just the icing. So bludgeon on and bludgeon deep! But keep bludgeoning. Increasing the angle on each successive bludgeon helps, too, if you can manage it. And if you want to hit it really hard as well, blast away, but you probably don't need to. An incessant, deep barrage of medium-paced strokes to the weak corner typically works just fine.

But right about now, you might be asking –

Won't hitting reliably and predictably to the opponent's weaker stroke in a match make it stronger?

As someone famous once said, "no." For starters, think of your own game. Does an opponent picking on a weakness in your game have the effect of making it better in a match? Well, it's the same for everybody else at every level of the game. Like Andy Murray's on-court mood, tennis vulnerabilities do *not* strengthen by being tested when points and games and sets are on the line.

Pummeling a weakness, making a player hit a deficient stroke over and over not only reveals its inadequacies to you, but it also reminds that player, as he or she repeatedly misses and miss-creates the shot of just how weak it is, too. Their confidence falters and the stroke in question gets even more questionable. If your simple bludgeon strategy is well executed and constructed effectively, it does not matter that the opponent knows it's coming. In fact, after a while, it positively helps.

## SOUL SEARCH AND RECOVERY

Not only does doubt creep into your opponent's suspect stroke, but there's a physical toll as well.

After every response shot the opponent makes, he or she has to try to recover to the center of the court or risk opening up the opposite corner for an easy winner. This recovery and reversing direction move, done two or three or four times per point gets harder to make as the opponent gets progressively more out of position on each relocation back to the corner and the center again. It's like a public radio fund drive – dogged, single-minded, and exhausting.

So, will a quality opponent just keep hitting to you and allowing you to put them in the same box canyon? Yes. Often, they will. And if they don't, you still get a prize. Stuck in an indefensible corner and losing ground on each set of steps back to that corner, many opponents will try to hit a hero shot to somehow turn things around. They may make a few of them, so say "nice shot" when they do, but on balance, their response shots will be ineffective and they will make errors trying to overcome your tactics with their desperate flailing force.

## THE VISIBLE HAND

Using patterns not only hikes up your score, it also polishes up your technique for the strokes in the pattern. And this is a valuable, over-looked add-on virtue.

Groundstrokes naturally want to go crosscourt, but going repeatedly to the backhand corner of a right-hander improves your *inside-out fore-hand*. And inside-out forehands boost the setup, turn, and direction of *all* of your forehands. Using the backhand corner pattern also fortifies your crosscourt backhands and inside-out and crosscourt short ball closing shots to boot.

And here's another positive – since you are controlling your oppo-nent's court movement and positioning by hitting a variety of shots to one location, your *aim* gets refined and improved as you go. Though your pattern hurts your opponent's strokes, hitting your shots to one place makes *your strokes* better in the course of a match.

And here's one more dividend you can collect on: Varying the strategy every so often away from the established pattern can also tally some well-earned easy points.

Once you've walloped your opponent into a strategic stupor, you can score easy winners by occasionally hitting *away from the pattern*. This works for all strokes including serves. Remember that no pattern works every time, and sometimes the opponent *does* make the hero shot and picks up a point or two. And sometimes you make an error. But if you're winning 7 out of 10 points going time and again after one stroke, it's a good strategy. So stay with it, and don't start thinking too much!

## APPROPRIATE OCCASIONS

That said, do always play smart tennis.

Decide on your strategy, but don't outsmart yourself by going to it before it's time. Let's assume you're using the backhand-corner pattern we've been discussing. Once you are provided with an opportunity to control the point, because of an opponent dished up short ball or weak ball, step in and hit as deep as possible to the backhand corner. Whether the response shot is a crosscourt backhand, a down-the-line backhand or maybe another mid-court piñata-pelota, drive it to the backhand corner again. If the opponent gets to this shot and sends it back, hit to the same corner again. Repeat until they make an error or you hit a winner. And they will. And *you* will.

And it all begins in that useless, but actually very useful, five minutes called the warm-up. (You did read that chapter, right?) Well, in case you didn't, here's a simple plan for extracting value from the warm-up.

Instead of being nervous or trying to correct an errant stroke of your own, distract and focus yourself by probing your opponent's game for their weakest stroke. Hit hard and soft and deep and short shots to their forehand and backhand and see what gives them the most problems.

Pick the stroke and start working it into your pattern as early as you can. Give it a few games and see if it succumbs to your evil intentions. If it does, stay the court. If not, still stay the court. Stick to the plan. Change plans only when your plan isn't working on more than 40-50% of the points. If that's happening, your pattern just *unfriended* you. (Sorry to use that term, too. But SEO, etc.)

And, again, even though we're bludgeoning, bludgeon with finesse. Wait patiently for an early invitation to do so.

Said another way –

Don't force your way into your chosen pattern if the opportunity is not really presenting itself. If your opponent hits one deep to your back-court and you need to send the ball back in the same direction or hit a recovery shot, just do that. The pattern may not get a fair chance to succeed if you can't start it on an advantageous opening. Recognize when you are hit these shots, and when you are not hit these shots.

And one more thing –

On those occasions when you've been using the pattern successfully and the opposite corner of el court is wide open, hit an easy winner to that location and be happy. Or, if a short ball opportunity presents itself and you can simply come up to the net and put the ball away, do that. Take the opportunities as they come, but work your pattern the rest of the time.

## FOREHAND COMPLEMENT

Once you develop a good bludgeon-the-backhand pattern, begin working on another pattern for days when your primary option isn't working and you need to go to the back-up.

Against some adversaries, this might mean picking on their forehand (*if* it's their weak stroke), or purposely offering up the short ball (if they net their approach shots or have a weak volley or just have no mobility). Luring a lumbering foe in with a short shot can sometimes be as effective as pinning him or her to a baseline corner. It's a longer run from the backcourt to the net than it is from the baseline center of the court to the baseline corner, and the total feet traveled to cover those dinker balls that they net or fence can add up to a distance that feels like miles over the course of a match.

And then there's the other side of the racquet: identifying your *opponent's patterns* and using them for your own evil ends. Figure out your opponent's patterns, then anticipate their moves and blunt their little bludgeon attempts by trying whenever possible not to let them start their sequence.

Of course, having and employing your own strong pattern also prevents your opponent from using theirs. In a way, match tennis could be described as "dueling patterns." And you want to be the one setting the terms of the duel; say, graphite blends at dawn, perhaps?

## WHEN CAN I START USING IT?

You can start using your pattern any time. Today is good.

## HOW DO I PRACTICE IT?

Every ball you hit, has to be hit *somewhere*, because, if you think about it, every ball is going to end up somewhere.

To hone your patterns, you need to practice with intent. Aim every practice shot somewhere *in particular*. Placement and tactics win tennis matches, and they rely on shot control. These exercises coupled with steady stroking and a positive outlook will help –

- Have a hitting partner feed balls to various locations on your court – both sides and all depths – and respond by hitting the ball to a cone target placed in the backhand corner.

- Variation: Same drill as above to the forehand corner.

- Serve, and during the ensuing point hit only to the backhand corner of your opponent's court.

- Return, and during the ensuing point hit only to the backhand corner of your opponent's court.

## PATTERN RECOGNITION

Become a connoisseur of tennis patterns.

As you watch matches live or on TV, collect players' patterns. Watch for their strengths and weaknesses and decide how you would play them and what one stroke you would attack if it were you out there on the court playing against them. Then, design the improved version of your own game around all the strokes needed for your pattern.

## AND NOW?

Watching a tennis match through the lens of patterns will change your view of your own game. It's like moving up to strategy hi-def. When your pattern's good, it's clear and glorious. When it's not, you'll see all the imperfections. Only in this case, make-up and lighting alone won't help. To make it look good, you need a sound game plan.

Every tennis game has patterns. Know yours. Develop yours. Make sure that the shot you're hitting is the shot you want to hit. And don't think too much out there.

## *ADDITIONAL INFORMATION PRESENTED AS A BONUS IN ORDER TO INCREASE PERCEIVED BOOK VALUE –*

Practice the shots you will use in your patterns.

Practice crosscourt rallies. Practice down-the-line rallies. Practice hitting two crosscourt shots and then hitting the third ball down the line. Aim for an area three feet inside the baseline and three feet inside the sidelines – deep, but with enough margin to make it hard for an anxious opponent to call it out and hard for you to hit out. Be specific about where the ball is going and know exactly how you'll make it go there.

Hit with room, but hit with precision. Improvisation can be thrilling in its uncertainty. *In theatre*. On the tennis court, improvisational stroking means you haven't practiced enough the shots you'll actually use to win. Your placement skills need to be on tap and solid so you can use your patterns without technique anxiety and even the hint of thrilling uncertainty.

# 7

# DANCING LIKE THE STARS

*"Dance, dance, dance."*
Steve Miller Band

There are three types of tennis players. Those who can hit and move. Those who can hit and not move as well. And those who are ranked below the first two.

In the pros, the first category features versatile players like Djokovic, Nadal, and Federer. In the second category are hard-hitting and hard-serving ones like Isner, Querrey, and Raonic. In the third are the ones on the outer courts.

All three categories contain great players, so it is clearly possible to win at the highest level without moving well. But the list of players who can hit *and* move features multiple Grand Slam winners – most of them with really schweet high-end watch endorsements.

At the pro level and every other level, moving well will take you farther faster.

## THE HAPPIEST PLACE ON COURT

The best strokes in the world won't be their best if your feet aren't taking your body to the right place to hit them.

Every shot you make on a tennis court has its *happy place* – a location on the court where your body and racquet are in el perfecto position to hit the ball with maximum contact, velocity, and direction. Early movement makes happy hitting happen.

By contrast, late movement to the ball puts you in the same situation as the slower moving pros, except without their overwhelming offensive weapons, big paydays, and courtesy cars. Without early, effective movement to the ball, you have to find ways to close points in the first few shots of a rally, land a high percentage of first serves, or rely on a steady stream of risky, low-percentage winners to compensate for weak positioning skills.

Late movement also makes players hesitant to set up points with multiple shots. Their games become hurried, harried, rushed, and uncertain. In short, outer court tennis.

## TO LIKE OR NOT TO LIKE

Tennis players, like athletes everywhere, tend to practice the skills they like to do and ones they do well already. (I may even have said that already.) It's comforting, comforting, and, well, comforting. If, for instance, you adore scorching you some forehands, you lavish time and attention on forehands and don't practice backhands. And I know I'm not telling you anything you don't know. But it's still the case.

Look around any tournament through the 5.0 level and it's obvious that this approach is widespread. There just aren't many well-balanced games out there. Although there are more than a few tournament hounds with massive, over-drilled forehands.

I'm sure this is obvious too, but repeatedly stating the obvious pays my mortgage: Practicing what you like makes your strong strokes stronger and your weaker strokes stagnant.

The formula is the same for movement work.

Most players would rather just whack orb than do drills to get better at moving to those orbs. Players neglect movement work because it lacks the glamour of walloping groundstrokes or clocking serves and takes more energy and effort in practice and more, well, movement.

What makes the pros the pros is their (sometimes coerced) willingness to practice and improve things they don't do well. That and their clothes, tans, and portfolios.


## TURNING PRO

The pros not only batter the ball harder and cleaner than we do, they do so because they move to the ball better – even the relatively slow ones. So how do the pros develop pro footwork and pro foot speed?

And does it happen automatically when you renounce your amateur status? Well, there's no doubt that realizing you have to win matches in order to eat *does* get your feet a pumpin', and fast. But for the pros it all starts way before that.

So, what's the pro difference? Well, a few things.

- Being told by coaches from the time you're 7 or 8 years old to move your feet between shots and recover to the center of the court quickly.

- Planning to move your feet between shots and recovering to the center of the court quickly.

- And, yes, you guessed it, *actually* moving your feet between shots and recovering to the center of the court quickly.

- Running distance training runs for match endurance.

- Running short training sprints for speed and quickness.

- Doing agility drills and other exercises on the tennis court and off that don't involve clobbering forehands or crushing serves.

- Getting into the best *lean* shape possible.

- Becoming more flexible – physically and emotionally, too, if necessary.

- Playing thousands of hours of tennis using pro footwork, even as an amateur.

- Deciding to and being told to get to every ball no matter what.

You may not have started playing at age seven or eight or had coaches relentlessly badgering you about correct form (or whatever form they were teaching) or scheduling those thousands of hours of matches for you. Or, maybe you have. But in any of the cases, you may still want better footwork. And you can have it! Here's how –

## BIG DECISIONS FIRST

Decide to be ready for every ball. Decide to get to every ball. Do not be deterred by errors, winners, your opponent's mood, or your own mood. Or the supermodel playing on court six.

## RETURN TO CENTAH

Concentrate on returning to the center of the court. Whether you impart strokes in front of the baseline or behind it, this patch of court is your, if you'll pardon the expression, ground of being. This is the place you want to plan to return to after each shot.

A lot has been written about the importance of an explosive first step, but you also need an *explosive second step*. The step that takes you back to center.

## A BOUNCE OF PREVENTION

To explode into your first and second steps, keep your feet light and chattering in micro-steps between shots. The best basketball, football, soccer, and tennis players are the best not only because of what they do when they have the ball, but also because of what they do when they *don't have the ball*. What goes on between shots is as important as the shots, and is what sets up the shots.

What are you doing between shots?

In tennis, unless you're hitting the ball, you have to keep moving. A tennis court is not a large area to defend unless you get a late start to the ball. Then it's huge. However, it doesn't take blinding foot speed to get to the ball quickly, just an idea of where it's going and a timely takeoff. So as soon as you hit your shot, start preparing for the return shot. Move back toward the center of the court and keep your feet bouncing.

Bounce before hitting. Bounce after hitting. Whenever you're not hitting, bounce. Constant, small foot movement keeps you ready to plant, push, and pursue. It also increases your ability to adjust your position if wind or spin moves the ball off course right before you hit it. And when you bounce, you should be bouncing on the front of your feet. The only time your feet should be flat on the court is when you're stepping in, planting your back foot before you step in, or shaking hands after your win.

And there's this.

A student recently passed along this unverified, but believable statistic – a typical pro player takes eight steps for every six steps a typical recreational player takes. In other words, pro players take more, smaller steps and keep their spacing options fluid, whereas recreational players often take fewer, bigger steps and end up unavoidably committing to flawed positioning because they haven't left themselves time or space to adjust.

As I've written in *Occam's Racquet* (my best-selling first book from seven years ago, that you probably have multiple copies of by now), you do want to connect to the court when you hit, but you don't want to connect too early or too close to the ball. A continuous flow of small steps helps you keep your options open.

## HIT AND TELLS

It's not all about you, though.

There's that opponent on the other side of the net and we need to know his or her intentions. You could just ask that individual where they're planning to hit their next shot, but many opponents won't tell you. Time to play poker. You see, getting to the ball early requires sound techniques and practice and the bounce, but it also requires anticipation, pattern recognition, and some good, educated guesses.

So, after you've hit your shot and you are springing nimbly up and down like a dashboard panda, you've only finished off part of the complete stroke sequence. After that, don't watch your shot, watch your opponent. Your ball will land where it will land. What matters now is where the follow-up shot from the other player will land. Watch your opponent's body and eyes for their tells.

As a match goes on, you can mentally catalog your opponent's tendencies. Once you see a pattern and figure out from the opponent's physical cues where the ball is headed, you can respond and move to cover the shot early and happily. Not too early. But happily is always fine.

You see, you have tells too. If you initiate your countermoves at the beginning of Mr. or Ms. Foe's stroke progression, you may tip him or her off that you've decoded their tendencies. If you're, like, totally obvious and give away the fact that you've broken their swing code, an alert opponent can develop sudden analytical abilities and just try to change tactics. And then you have to start the whole process over again. So be sly. Wait until the other player focuses their eyes on the ball right before contact to make your countermove.

You don't need to be Usain Bolt to move better and win more often: just an observant, analytical bouncing version of you. A version who is willing to apply more energy and process to their match tennis.

## DAS WORK

And, of course there are drills you can add to your practice sessions and matches to not only build your skills, but also to tire you out more than before you read this chapter –

**Follow The Ball**. Your hitting partner is at the net with a ball. You're at the baseline in the ready position with your bounce going. Move in whatever direction the person holding a ball at the net directs you to go. Do this for five minutes.

**Four Square**. Your hitting partner stands at mid-court on their side of the net with a hopper of balls. You are at the center of the baseline. Your partner hits a shot to either your deep forehand or backhand or your mid-court forehand or backhand. Move to get each shot and then move back to the center to recover. Fantastic drill. Fantastic exercise.

You can also, without negative consequences –

• **Increase Your Flexibility.**
Find stretches that are comfortable for you and stretch your quads, hamstrings, groin, hips, and calves *every day*. Stretch dynamically before you play or work out and statically after you play or work out.

And you should additionally –

• **Warm Up Fully.**
Don't start a match with cold muscles. Before or match or workout, jog lightly for 10 minutes. Stretch your lower *and* upper body.

• **Warm Down Fully.**
Follow a post-match stretching routine to prevent soreness.

• **Enjoy Life Fully.**

Goes without saying.

And it's not a bad idea to –

## SOME OBSERVATION –

Watch the pros – the fast and the slow – on TV, or, live, if you have the opportunity and cash. And for a few games in each match, watch only their feet and see how much the pros move between shots and how small their set up steps are.

Bottom darn line on the whole movement portion of the game of tennis?

The best strokes in the world can't be their best, or inflict you some The FOING, if you're not in the best place to stroke them strokes. And the best way to ensure you can arrive early and often?

## AND MAYBE THE SIMPLEST AND HARDEST SUGGESTION OF ALL –

Lose weight.

The best way to get those explosive first, second, and third steps, enjoy better movement at all times and have fewer back, joint, and health problems is to shed unnecessary el-bees. Tennis is not a game of weightlifter strength or sprinter speed. It *is* very much a game of flexibility, stamina, and quick reflexes.

Extra weight slows you down and tires you out. The best of the current crop of players are lean and agile. You can be too. Live longer and happier. Look great in swimwear. Turn heads at the doctor's office. The pros shouldn't have all the fun.

### ADDITIONAL INFORMATION PRESENTED AS A BONUS IN ORDER TO INCREASE PERCEIVED BOOK VALUE –

Work out smart.

To improve your game, you don't necessarily need to practice more than you do now, but you may need to allot your time a lot differently.

If, for instance, you're losing matches because you fatigue, because your legs can't get your body to the right place on the court and keep those legs under you when you need to get low, you should spend more time on fitness and less time on strokes. It's just smart tennis time management. It's not about spending more hours (who has those?) on tennis, it's about spending the hours you have on the parts of your game that will help you the most.

What parts are those for you?

# 8

# COMMITMENT ISSUES

*"There's no abiding success without commitment."*
Tony Robbins

It's June 30, 2011, Centre Court, Wimbledon and Maria Sharapova has a big problem. Battling Sabine Lisicki for a spot in the finals, Maria can't get her serve in. *Really* can't get it in. Things are bad – Shaquille-from-the-free-throw-line bad. Moon launch toss. Speed bump swing. Rollercoaster shoulder dips. Her motion looks like a conflicted wind-mill taking a stage bow. She double faults 13 times in 66 serve points, gets in just 48% of her first serves and 21 of 34 second serves. But here's the serve kicker – *the big problem doesn't stop her*. She beats Lisicki 6–4, 6–3 and grits her way into the finals.

And it wasn't just at SW19, as they call it.

Maria scuppered a fleet of first and second serves in a worldwide armada of matches in 2010 and 2011, but still won often and steered a mostly steady course back up the WTA rankings. Double-faulting 13 times in the Wimbledon semi isn't a recommended method for match success (Sharapova also *lost* plenty of matches at the hand of her serve), but Maria's way of dealing with her serve problems is.

So, what's Maria doing right when things are going wrong, and how can we do it, too? And would it have helped Shaq?

## POSITIVE COMMITS

Statistically, the serve is the most important stroke in match tennis, but as Maria proved, even terrible numbers don't necessarily doom a player and her chances. And good numbers don't always spell the "w." In losing that same semi, Lisicki made only four double faults and served harder than Sharapova in the bargain. Clearly, there must be something else *more* important for winning matches than even the most important stroke. There is, and Maria is the wealthy, famous, living proof. It's not a stroke.

It's an attitude: *Commitment*.

Specifically, commitment to each stroke you hit, regardless of the situation, the opponent, or the score. This is what Maria's doing right.

Maria Sharapova is a great champion, a tenacious competitor, and not a bad dresser, either. In her best years before her 2016 doping suspension, she rarely let another player into her game physically *or* let her own difficulties affect her mentally. She stayed committed to her game when things were going well *and* when things were *not* going so well. This is how she won even when betrayed a faltering, spazzy serve. Her wayward serve is a classic recreational stroke issue, but her solution is pure professional.

Recreational players typically flounder during stroke storms. But the pros can't afford to let a one-shot tsunami capsize their game. Except for the occasional mandatory plane catching, sandbagging, or mood swing, they stay committed to their game and their strokes. How? Rigorous practice, sports shrinks, and a lot of staff to pay. It's simply too expensive to space out.

Watch a pro match and take notice, not just of the socks, the teeth, and the amount of employees and celebrities in the player's box, but of how the pros *commit* to their shots. Even when a pro is going to hit the most ill-advised shot of the Open Era or a routine open court winner blast, they hit every shot with focus, purpose, conviction, and a fresh overwrap. Watch a recreational match, and see how often a player waffles on a shot and eats the point.

As my teenhood buddy's father used to say, "Whenever you're asked a question in business, give a definite answer. You can always change your mind later." The confidence that decisiveness and resolve inspire in others and, more importantly, *in ourselves*, can help us through some rough times. And a balky serve.

Commit to the shot. You can always change your mind in the same situation in the future.

## THE ROAD NOT NOT TAKEN

The Oxford American Dictionary defines commitment as: "*Dedication.*

*Application.*" And, "*An engagement or obligation that restricts freedom of action.*"

So commitment is positive, but it's also negative. Positive because you go through with what you started. Negative because you *don't* go through with something else. But even this negative, restrictive side is positive for tennis matches. Restricting freedom of action on the court (by cutting out too many on-court decisions and revisions) is a good thing. And for a good reason.

Tennis is mostly a reactive game.

We fully control the serve, but as we've seen with a certain female player of Russian descent, the fact that we can proactively produce that stroke doesn't always help. When you're in the flow of a point, there's not much time to run options and none at all to rework your technique. You need to know what you're going to do and then do it with intention and conviction. Any doubt that distracts you from this quick, dynamic reaction hurts your ability to make good strokes and points. And impedes your match path to accruing you some The FOING.

Everyone lacks something. You may crack groundies, but crack up at the net. You may hit all your lead-up shots like a general, but fumble like a new recruit at set point. You may hit heartily against lesser players, but wimp out against the bigs. But none of those tendencies dooms your match game if you, as my jazz band director in high school used to say, "Make your mistakes loud."

In a word – *Commit*.

Then you know what to work on. Commit to your shots; your winners *and* your errors. And if something's goes toxic, seal it off and keep the damage contained.

## COMPARTMENT HEAD

In 2010 and 2011, Maria Sharapova saved more matches than you can shake a sponsored stick at by committing fully to her game *as it was that day*. She *cordoned off* the problem stroke (yes, her serve) on *each point*, and *after each point*, and didn't let it spill over to her other strokes *in that point*, or to *other points*. She might have wanted to tinker with her motion or her toss during the match – watching at home, I know *I* did – but this would only have made things worse.

Not only would her serve not have been working, not only would the correction probably not have helped, but the distraction caused by the attempted correction would have *thrown off her other strokes as well*. Instead, she committed to playing with the flawed stroke she had and won the necessary points *in other ways*. The *practice court* is truly the only place for a wholesale correction like the one Maria needed.

Without the analytic shut down of the fight-or-flight match brain, you can spend time and repetitions making a smart, lasting fix. Of course, all good match players *adjust* during a match (Nadal and his shorts, for instance), but adjusting is different than *revising*. As my previously quoted golf pro friend, Zach, once sagely counseled, "No swing thoughts on the golf course." (Or on the tennis court for that matter. Especially if they're *golf* swing thoughts.)

Contrast this with tennis as played by the 99%. In this larger world of players, egos often stay wounded from that mishit shot two points or two games or one set ago. Worse still, players want lesson-worthy perfection on the court and derail the good stuff they are doing by lamenting and fretting about every error *while the ball is still in play*. The pros know that the only fact that really matters is: *Did the shot go in?* And then, *what's the opponent doing with the ball now?* And only later, *how many ranking points was I defending?* Regret costs you. Resolve rewards you.

And, like, remember: *The only important shot in tennis is the one you're about to hit.*

## DENIABLE PLAUSIBILITY

Committing to commitment takes commitment.

Wimbledon semis or the challenge court at the club, keep your commitment to commitment by praising yourself for all your good shots and *ignoring the bad ones.* The great golfer, Jack Nicklaus, once said, "I've never missed a three-footer." Of course that's not literally true, Jack missed three-foot putts. Even the greatest golfer of all time can't jar everything. He also said when asked to describe a short putt that didn't drop, "I made that one, it just didn't go in."

So what did he mean?

What Jack meant in both cases was this – if you hit it right, you hit it right *and* you'd hit it the same way again the next time and all the times after that. In tennis too, once you have your stroke and your method, you don't doubt it. You commit to it and do it. And ignore the outcome when it isn't good, and move on to the next point. Jack wasn't being delusional, he was being a champion. Champions (as my teen-hood friend's apocryphal dad suggested) win by believing they're champions, regardless of how they're hitting on one particular day.

Adopting Jack's extremely short-term, amnesiac view of mistakes helps open your mind to stroke commitment. If you let your mind dwell on mistakes that have already happened, they will take over your current shots. Forget the bad shots. Just get ready to hit the next one.

A short-term, narrow view into the *future* helps too. Don't obsess over the mistakes you *may* make, either, okay? Assume success and deny the rest.

This doesn't mean, by the way, that simply hitting shots with conviction or willfully blocking out errors will make technically flawed strokes technically better. That kind of improvement only happens through practice, dedication to proper technique, and a cash windfall. You can bet that Jack practiced a lot of those three-footers he "never missed" and Maria probably spent $10^{16}$ or something hours trying to tame her disobedient serve. *Just not during a competition.*

## PRACTICING COMMITMENT

Maria Sharapova is the poster girl for commitment, fortitude, success, and Nike, Canon, and Cole Haan. It's what you get when you have to prove yourself on court at a young age, in a new country and a tough environment, with uncertain serve instruction.

However, Maria's way is *not* the only way to find mental fortitude. It's possible to gain confidence simply through stroke competence and the use of on-court compartmentalization. Emigration is optional. But, like Maria, we need to face the facts and go into every match and compete with the game we have. The first step then is to figure out what that game is.

## CHECKING FOR LEAKS

Which of your strokes distracts *you* from the game you want to play? Take an inventory of all your strokes to find which ones fill you with something less than full confidence. Make these better and boost your level of competence.

Once you do the analysis, it's time for practice –

**Trouble Ball –**
Somewhat like the golf drill, "worst ball." Select your weakest shot and during a practice rally, try to respond to every ball *with this shot*. For instance, if you don't like your backhand volley, take every deep ball, mid-court ball, and volley from the backhand side and try to volley it.

**Russian Around –**
There is some good that can come from Maria's troubles. This exercise for one. Hit only one serve per practice point and make it a weak second serve. As you play the point out, make adjustments to the rest of your game knowing that your serve will *not* carry the day. No need to toss too high, lose your timing, or drop your head, though.

After all or some of that, it's time to court test it. Play a practice match where you score, but where you don't worry about the score (a good exercise on its own) and hit every shot like you mean it.

## NATURAL OR NURTURAL?

It's been said that you can't coach height. Or innate talent. Or most of the players on tour. But you can coach *yourself* on commitment. Starting today.

Be Maria 2011. Embrace your inner, early-decade Sharapova.

Complete and accelerate each stroke and use your lower body. Stay within your game and refocus after every point. Have a private turned-to-the-fence conference with your fist pump. Hit each shot and live with the consequences. If the ball goes long, stay in your game. If you hit absolutely the wrong shot, stay in your game. If you have to switch racquet endorsements for financial or philosophical reasons, stay in your game.

Commit. And, I may have already said this, stay in your game.

Have faith in what you're doing no matter how it's going or if your opponent shrieks even shriller than you do. Always hit like you mean it and carry yourself like a winner. Play each match with resoluteness, resolve, and fearlessness.

Oh, and work on your serve.

### *ADDITIONAL INFORMATION PRESENTED AS A BONUS IN ORDER TO INCREASE PERCEIVED BOOK VALUE –*

Commit to using new tennis balls.

Every time you play.

Previously-played tennis balls don't fly as straight as new balls (because the cover wears unevenly), reduce your stroke and serve speed (because they lose pressure), and look grody to the max (because they're dingy and disgusting).

Don't be cheap. Have some pride. Commit to your own tennis success in every possible way. Make your game the best it can be. Use new tennis balls.

# SECTION III

## POSTPLAY

# 1

## TAKE A MOMENT

*"Wait a minute, Mr. Postman."*
– Georgia Dobbins, et al.

Okay, so your match is finished, what do you do now?

First of all, let's hope that the following is true. Or substantially true. Or may be true at some point in the future if you can just carve out a little time for yourself away from lesser obligations like family, job, and community. (Just kidding, of course. Basically.)

But back to the main (as the kids these days say) *narrative*. By now, if you've read and implemented the preceding carefully researched, exhaustively thought-out, lovingly scriven chapters in this, my second tennis instructional book, you have improved your strokes, and your equipment, and your fitness, and your mental preparation.

And when you played that real-world match play adversary, you entered the match court with a plan, warmed up correctly, paused before you hit the ball, anticipated and practiced for the off-pace opponent, were conscious of your movement, and committed to every shot.

And, so, assuming that all of that or a big part of it is true, what's left to do? Not a whole lot, really. More or less just one simple, not so simple task –

Take
Another
Moment.

[THE REST OF THIS PAGE INTENTIONALLY LEFT BLANK, SO YOU
WILL TAKE THAT MOMENT]

Yes, you saw it right. The last order of business on the court after any match is to *take another moment*.

But not just the standard kind of empty, aimless moment.

Instead, you want to observe a thoughtful, considered interval between the end of your just completed match and dinner, or errands, or work commitments, or whatever else you, as a busy, modern, successful person, need to accomplish.

So don't leave the court just yet. Stand in one place, take a couple breaths, and let a little more time pass.

You see, while it's technically true that you're done playing, it's also true that you're still not quite done with your game.
Even after I've taken *the moment*?

Yes, even after that.

You see, after the taken moment is good and observed, there's this optional but not actually optional add-on: the really-taking-in-the-situation reflective interval. Look up, or down, or wherever you look during reverential intervals, and give a nod to whatever or whomever you give nods to for the pleasure and blessing of a day playing tennis. The blessing of being on a court, and exercising, and doing your body and your spirit a favor.

This isn't nothing and it's important to acknowledge, however briefly, your favorable situation in the universe and your admirably active life. And maybe your nicely defined quads and forearms as well.

But even beyond those bounties, there are still a couple more items to attend to in the much more prosaic jots-and-tittles department.

After the quiet thanks and contemplation, drop down a few chakras and get all basic and specific. Take another moment or two to inventory yourself and your equipment. Ask your post-match self – is anything impaired or compromised in either sector?

Did a string break? Did your overwrap or grip wear out? Do you need new sunscreen or lip block? Do you need a bigger water bottle? Or another towel? Or another racquet? Or a spare shirt?

Or, and also –

Did you sustain any strains or injuries? And, if you did, have you decided how (not *if*) you want to take care of them?

Take stock of the physical plant, the tangible entity that is you the player, and be always thoughtful about how you can make it better and more effective. And how to best prepare it for next time.

Mindfulness is an overused (and kind of pyschobabbly and squishy) term, but it's what we're talking about here.
Mindfulness. Or, if you haven't quite filled that in yet, then – Mndflnss.

Which leads me to wonder – does the invoking of that trendy word put this humble book not only in the Amazon search categories of tennis, sports, instruction, coaching, philosophy, humor, self-aggrandizement, but in "self-help" as well? Time will tell, I suppose.

Anyway, give yourself time to review yourself and your gear physically before regular life resumes. And think about them both before you leave the court.

Really.

Why?

Because everyday life will squeeze those concerns out of your exquisite, tennis-centric brain ten minutes after you drive, or bike, or have your driver take you away from the court. That's what everyday life does. And it does it well. And it doesn't care about your tennis. But we do.

If you are serious about winning, these parts of your game – your tennis infrastructure – must be skillfully and diligently managed. Every part matters to the whole that is your game.

But there's even another reason.

Not rushing *after* the match is valuable in the same way as not rushing *before* the match is. Maintain your personal tempo. Don't let your everyday self and your everyday life push your tennis self and your tennis life around.

And, besides, remember that you are playing a sport for your enjoy-ment, so it's okay to bask in that enjoyment for a few moments after you finish playing. The game doesn't end when the last point is won. It ends when you have properly done everything before, during, and after the match that you need to do. And when you've –

Taken.
Another
Moment.

And after you do, and you're really done with your tennis time, slowly head to your conveyance home. But, please, don't be too quick to let the world in again. It's not going anywhere. And since I wasn't completely, exhaustively, and rigorously forthcoming about the end-of-match ministrations, you still have a couple more, really small things to do anyway. But we'll get to them in the next chapter.

## ADDITIONAL INFORMATION PRESENTED AS A BONUS IN ORDER TO INCREASE PERCEIVED BOOK VALUE –

Why are we always rushing?

We spend all week waiting for our time on the court, and then when the match is done, we rush on to the next thing. It doesn't have to be this way. You can slow it all down. You can appreciate the moment. You can take a moment. You don't need to be a monk. Or a nun. Or a yogi. You can still be in the world. You can even be of the world.

No one's making you rush. You can set your own tempo.

Just remember – every day is a precious day of your life that you'll never get back. We all are partners in the cosmic dance. Soak it in. Revel in it. Feel the rhythm. Don't move on too quickly. Please. Enjoy the good things. And just enjoy the things.

As they say in that ad, "One life, right? Don't blow it."

# THE SIXTH SET

*"We can take care of some of that."*
– Billy Bob Thornton, *Armageddon*

Hello again.

I think I know what you're thinking. You're thinking that after you focused on your post-match moments, took your personal inventory, and conveyed yourself to your beautiful house with your beautiful spouse (or whatever living 'arrangement,' as the French would say, that you're, like, in), that you were done with the whole attend-thoughtfully-to-the-match-process business from beginning to end. Well, not quite. There's still the sixth set to take care of.

The *sixth set?*

Yeah, sorry. There's one more last last thing. But it's important. And necessary. Like the 19th hole in golf, the sixth set in tennis is potentially as significant as the five sets you just won at the club. The sixth set is where you mend, refuel, analyze, and plan for upcoming victories.

So far, if you've followed the steps to fill in your game gaps, you've done what needed to be done to compete against an opponent. And implement you some The FOING. But now that you've played a match, it's time to use that experience to inform and improve your game for your next outing.

Yes, there's still a little more to do. But this really is the final task in remaking your match tennis game. At least as far as this, my second book, goes. So, without any more extra nouns or verbs of any kind, here is the mercifully brief after-play list –

## THE LIST

The after-play list in three short steps.

Step One – Once home from the match, stretch the relevant and affected muscle groups and take a shower.

Step Two – Enjoy some post-match recovery food.

Step Three – After you're clean and you've taken care of your body and refueled your brain, it's time for the step you've been waiting for – the last one. And the last step is –

**The Post-Matchums.**

This is the critical how-did-it-go-today breakdown. The time to make some notes and express some thoughts to yourself about your just completed performance on the match court.

Your post-matchum can be just a few lines, but it's important to write something. Writing makes real what you may have been doing unthinkingly. And it gives you a record of what you did, how you were feeling when you did it, and how well what you did worked. If it sounds better, you can call it a diary, or an after action report, or even an ocelot. Just write some notes and reflections in it, whatever it's called.

And –

If you were fortunate enough to have had someone chart your match for you, this is the time to review the chart and incorporate that statistical information into your post-matchum, or diary, or after-action, or ocelot. Or whatever. Because here's the main thing – you don't want to let the match you just played go by and sail off into some little-used corner of the memory file unacknowledged. If you're truly serious about improving your match results in the future, you need to tell yourself about what you thought of what you did and how you performed today.

And lastly, once you've analyzed your plan and its success or shortcomings, write down for yourself any strokes you need to concentrate on, and what strategies you want to keep or modify.

I know what you're thinking. I really do.

You're thinking that this all sounds like a lot of extra, tedious, inconvenient work, and maybe the last thing you want to do after a hard-fought on-court duel, and a stretch, and a shower, and some, I don't know, Lobster Thermidor tacos, or something. You just wanted to smack the sphere, conquer the foe, and go home and *not* write about it.

However, if you want to win and keep winning and moving up in skill level, you need to get past after match summations such as, "I won today," or "I sucked felt today," or "Yeah, it went okay." Not one of these statements gives you any actionable information that will help you improve. However, it's often what I hear from players when I ask them to describe their match performance.

Like great comedy, your after-match report to yourself, your post-matchum if you will, needs to be *specific*. And timely.

If you won, *how* did you do it? What strokes and strategies worked?

If you thought you played terribly, *be specific* about what you mean by that characterization.

Just like there's no day where all parts of your game worked flawlessly, there's likewise no day where everything *didn't* work. Really. Despite how crushing any loss may be, not everything you did was terrible. And a *general* description of the day on the court doesn't tell you anything about what to improve or what to throw out.

There are negatives in any win, and positives in any loss. I'm not saying you need to sugarcoat anything or butter yourself up or deny any realities. But at the same time, don't be a rapidly cycling bipolar tennis head case, either. For one thing, that's no way to separate yourself from the mass of other players out there. Be thee instead clear-eyed about your triumphs and your defeats so that you can maintain your composure and secure more triumphs. Be thee also descriptive and specific about what happened or risk resigning your results to one of two meaningless categories above.

And you didn't read this whole book to end up there, did you?

Even though this is the final step, it's just as vital to your match game success as any other step.

So, please, follow through. Take the final step. Write down in your ocelot specifically what worked and what didn't work and what you were feeling and how your energy was and what you need to work on, and you're done.

Done.

You're really done. You made it. You've taken all the steps to fill in the gaps in your game-game and make yourself a better player.

So now relax, do whatever it is you want to do with the rest of your day, and then get some sleep.

There are always more matches to be played. And your body and mind and spirit need to be ready.

The FOING awaits!

*ADDITIONAL INFORMATION PRESENTED AS A BONUS IN ORDER TO INCREASE PERCEIVED BOOK VALUE –*

Practice often. Play well. Have fun.

# SECTION IV

# A PEN DISSE(E)S

# 1

## I RATE

*"I think people make way too much of ratings."*
– Walter Cronkite

The tennis powers have tried for almost forty years to develop a broadly-accepted handicap system that might possibly, someday, if used correctly and not perverted by typical human ingenuity and pluck, ensure that players of similar abilities compete against one another in a transparent and accepted format.

And how's that working out so far?

Well, here's where we sit in 2018 in the quest to develop one system that everyone will go by:

We have three.

*And* one additional offering of my own design unveiled for the first time in this book. Why not? It's *my* book.

So then, all told, at present, here's the laundry list of tennis handicapping systems. There's the USTA's National Tennis Rating Program (NTRP) rating system, the ITN (International Tennis Number) system, the newer UTR (Universal Tennis Rating) system, and my own Cootsona Binary Rating (CBR) system. And if I were more diligent about researching this nether part of my second book, I'm sure I could probably find a few more. In any case, here are the main tennis handicapping schemes –

## NATIONAL TENNIS RATING PROGRAM (NTRP) RATINGS SYSTEM

The most commonly used ratings system for league and tournament play in the U.S. Players are rated from 1.0 (just beginning) to 7.0 (ATP/WTA touring professional).

(https://assets.usta.com/assets/639/15/National%20tennis%20Rating%20Program.pdf)

## INTERNATIONAL TENNIS NUMBER (ITN) SYSTEM

Not sure where this one is used. However, it does snug up to the NTRP chart as a sidebar. In any case, we increase to ten levels in this one, in an inverted order. 1 is a tour-level felt-whacker. 10 is a player who is just beginning to make meaningful contact with said felt.

(https://assets.usta.com/assets/639/15/National%20tennis%20Rating%20Program.pdf)

## UNIVERSAL TENNIS RATING (UTR) SYSTEM

Number of levels up to 16. (This *must* be a very good system. More levels *have* to be better.) In this algorithmic blend of player skills, match wins, and competition faced, 1.0 is a beginner, 16.5 is king or queen of the tour. By the way, as of this writing, Roger Federer is a 16.25. Wonder what it takes to get that last quarter point…

(https://myutr.com)

## COOTSONA BINARY RATING (CBR) SYSTEM

Two levels (both stolen from my golf pro friend, Zach). Those who play for money. Those who don't.

## WHERE DO YOU STAND?

The NTRP system is an interesting blend. The lower levels of the chart assess a player's rating based on the skills they have, while the last few levels promote a player based on competitive results. All of which was probably the right way to structure it: past a certain point of stroke development, the only relevant criteria for moving up is match success. Fine. However, as most of you who have played USTA league tennis know, all the ratings from 3.0 upward are all essentially based on competitive success. (You've all no doubt *seen* some of the incomplete games out there.) It may be that the application of the system has changed the system. Like Heisenberg petting Schrödinger's cat. Or something.

I just don't know what to say about the ITN ratings. Having taken their online test, it seems that this framework is simply a revisionist tweak of the NTRP version with slightly more nuanced questions. Done in reverse. And made global. Or something.

The UTR is intriguing. Not yet widely accepted, its blend of match results and weighting of opponents has implications for the ATP and WTA rankings and could produce a dynamic system that would make week-to-week professional tournament results more vital to casual fans. But here's a question: Does Tennis want the added interest, money, and new players this could provide? It would go a long way toward removing the impenetrability of the current rankings system, and would almost qualify as a move toward marketing our sport to the public. Is this a step the governing bodies could bring themselves to take? Stay tuned.

As far as my CBR system is concerned, what more can be said?

## WHAT DOES IT ALL MEAN?

You can be *in* the ratings but you don't have to be *of* the ratings. Know the ratings if you need to, but don't forget to enjoy our beautiful game.

# 2

## TENNCOMIUMS

*"I always pass on good advice. It is the only thing to do with it. It is never any use to oneself."*
— Oscar Wilde

An *encomium* is defined as "Warm praise for a person or thing."

A *tenncomium* is defined as "Warm praise for a thing that might personally help your tennis."

Here then, in no particular order that I can figure, are helpful statements I find myself mouthing (or thinking about mouthing) on the teaching court from time to time –

- Work on your serve.
- Great volleyers are great half-volleyers.
- If you're pushed deep, respond deep.
- If everything about a serve feels right, but it nets, you looked down too soon.

- Don't rush yourself.
- The only things you want to do fast in tennis are moving to the ball and setting up to hit it.
- Start your groundstroke preparation as soon as you know what stroke you're going to hit.
- It doesn't matter so much how fast you move to recover after a shot, it matters how quickly you start to recover.
- If you're hitting your maintenance shots at 60%, don't hit your closing shots at 90%. Try 80%. You'll land more in.
- Better yet, hit at 60 – 75% most of the time.
- Work on your serve.
- Slower swings with center contact produce more pace than faster swings with edge contact.
- Re-characterize what a winner is. More angle, less pace.
- When you go for the coup de grâce shot, do these things no matter what the bounce height is – pick your target, bend your knees, look at the contact, and don't check the target.
- On overheads, see the ball hit the strings and don't hit harder than 50%.
- Make the opponent move.
- On groundstrokes, hit the ball at the top of the bounce.
- On serves, hit the ball at the top of the toss.
- Make sure your shoes are tied.
- Work on your serve.
- Practice long rallies.
- Practice shot combinations until they become habits. Inventing them during a match is distracting. To you.
- Forget bad shots quickly.
- Remember what you did right.
- Make sure you have a place to put the second ball when you serve. You may need it.
- Always start serving with two balls in your possession.
- If you net your first serve and the ball rolls out onto the court, clear it before you hit your second serve.
- Call the score before you serve.
- Don't worry about how weird the opponent looks.

- Don't fixate on the opponent's weird strokes.
- Don't covet the opponent's boyfriend or girlfriend. Or dog.
- Work on your serve.
- Don't win by cheating. Even a little.
- 99% out is 100% good.
- Win by playing better than the opponent.
- Learn how to feed the ball to start the rally.
- Learn how to warm up in the short court.
- Hit as many of the bad shots as you can before you begin the match.
- Play like you're two inches shorter than you are.
- Run low when you go to the net. Stay low when you get there.
- Stay low on the baseline.
- Don't stay low on the serve.
- Work on your serve.
- Become a great serve returner.
- Fast serves come back fast. Serve slower if you can't recover in time for the follow-up shot.
- Very few players have lost by being consistent. Unless it's by being consistently wild.
- Know why you're hitting the shot you're hitting.
- Hit the shot you're hitting.
- Play your way into a match. Start at ¾ speed. Get a lot of balls in. Build your confidence and increase your pace as you go.
- You don't need to use up all your errors right away. Spread them out.
- Don't make all the mistakes for your opponent. Make them work for their points.
- Always try to keep your overheads in front of you, and not over your head.
- Serve returns are hit with your weight more than with your swing. Take a short backswing, step in, and complete the stroke.
- On groundstrokes, you want a backswing, a step, and a

follow-through. If there's not enough time for all three, step
and follow-through. If there's only time enough for one,
follow-through.

- No matter how bad your position and set up are for a
  groundstroke, a follow-through alone can often save the
  stroke.
- "Ball don't lie." The flight of your shot will tell you most
  everything about how you hit it. The spin on the ball will tell
  you the rest.
- Don't forget the dropshot.
- Work on your serve.
- Tournament tennis is strong medicine. You will learn quickly
  whether you love it or hate it.
- Tennis nirvana is finding a group of like-minded and like-
  skilled individuals and meeting for a weekly doubles game.
- Start your volleys with your arms forward and your racquet
  ahead of your feet. Take no backswing. Step in and drive the
  racquet forward and level.
- On volleys at head height or below, keep the racquet head at
  eye level.
- Make all volley adjustments with your body. Keep the
  racquet angle and wrist position constant.
- Don't swing the racquet on volleys below net level. Be the
  backboard. Let the angle of the racquet face create loft and
  net clearance.
- Get your racquet back into two hands after every stroke.
  Even winners.
- The fewer grip switches, the better.
- Love to land the ball in the court.
- Go for everything.
- Work on your serve.
- Measure the net before a match with a tape measure. It
  should be 36" on center. You'll make your opponent wonder.
- Keep the ball away from the middle of your opponent's
  court at mid-depth. Hit an angle or hit it deep.
- Stay in the pattern until you can break the pattern.

- Check your shoulders for tension. Relax them.
- Use the lightest hand pressure you can manage.
- Keep your feet moving between shots. Even just a little.
- Watch the ball into contact. After you've made your shot, look at your opponent.
- You don't need to actively dislike your opponent, but it can help.
- Tennis can be played angry.
- Tennis can be played happy.
- Tennis can be played relaxed.
- Don't play tennis tense.
- You don't have to buy what your opponent is selling.
- Tennis is not really about big, hard swings. Use your weight for power. Let the racquet work for you.
- Work on your serve.
- Tennis strokes are precise. They need to be done exactly right, not approximately right. Precise, repeatable form matters.
- Racquet face control is a key to shot placement.
- Shot placement is a key to winning.
- Winning is a key to winning more.
- All other things being equal, winning more is better than winning less.
- Work on your serve.
- Practice often. Play well. Have fun.
- And work on your serve.

# ABOUT THE AUTHOR

Marcus Cootsona is a tennis teaching professional, a contributor to *Inside Tennis*, and a member of the Wilson Advisory Staff. Tennis is his life. He has written a tennis novel you should also probably add to your sports-lit library – *Slammin', A Wally Wilson Mystery* – exclusively available as a free bonus to those brave enough to join his mailing list. Sign up here!

*Tnns Lssns* is the follow-up to *Occam's Racquet – 12 Simple Steps to Smarter Tennis* and that book is highly recommended as a way to learn the basics of Marcus' need-to-know teaching philosophy and combine the mental and physical games to improve your tennis.

If you enjoyed *Tnns Lssns*, please consider leaving a review on Amazon (or Goodreads). Even something short or very short or

extremely short would be incredibly helpful: Amazon US |
Goodreads.

Please feel free to get in touch on Facebook, or send Marcus an email
at: myprotennis@comcast.net. He will answer you personally.

All the Best,

Marcus.

Printed in Great Britain
by Amazon

83005610R00119